Tableau Step-by-Step for Beginners

Arshad Khan

Tableau Step-By-Step for Beginners
Arshad Khan
California, USA

Table of Contents

About the Author

Arshad Khan is a versatile BI professional with over 30 years of experience. He has consulted for Accenture, PwC, Deloitte, Chevron, Bose Corporation, Daimler Chrysler, Genentech, PepsiCo, Hitachi-America, and many other blue-chip companies. Mr. Khan is currently working as a self-service analytics consultant for UCSF. Previously, he consulted for the Navy as a BI Architect, implemented an analytics project at ABB Digital, and also led numerous analytics projects at Juniper Networks.

Mr. Khan has 15 books to his credit, including six books on BI/analytics. He has taught at 7 universities including Golden Gate University and the University of California (Berkeley, Santa Cruz, and San Diego). Mr. Khan has a graduate degree in engineering and an MBA.

Preface

Tableau Step-by-Step for Beginners provides an introduction to Tableau, which is the leading data visualization software. The exercises contained in it cover the functions most widely used by business users. After completing these exercises, users will be able to develop simple reports and dashboards and, also, perform basic analysis. The skills developed through these exercises will become the foundation for those who want to become experts in the use of Tableau software for reporting, analysis and data visualization.

Tableau Step-by-Step for Beginners contains a total of 35 exercises. Out of these, one describes the Tableau interface. The other 34 exercises demonstrate, in a step-by-step manner, various functions such as filtering, drilldown, sorting, swapping, aggregating, trending, and formatting. These exercises show how to work with and manage workbooks, export results to Excel or PDF, and also display, download and export data. Also covered are various analysis functions such as Top N and forecasting.

Tableau Step-by-Step for Beginners also demonstrates how to quickly develop a dashboard and customize it by incorporating quick filters and layout formatting.

Introduction: Getting Ready

This book is based on Tableau version 2019-2-0, which was released on May 21, 2019.

The following three steps need to be followed in order to install Tableau and download two spreadsheets (which will be required for the 35 hands-on exercises in this book):

Step 1: Download Tableau version 2019-2-0 from this link:
https://drive.google.com/open?id=1qPhpp5cxdSKuAckhFMQXZUtIfpvB2efS

If this link is broken, which can happen over time due to a number of reasons, send an e-mail to akhan95129@gmail.com to obtain an updated link.

Alternate Tableau download site: https://www.tableau.com/support/releases/desktop/2019.2#esdalt

Step 2: Install Tableau by double-clicking on the installation file (*TableauDesktop-64Bit-2019-2-0*), which was downloaded in Step 1.

Step 3: Download two Excel spreadsheets, ***Sample – Superstore*** and ***Global Superstore***, from this link:
https://drive.google.com/open?id=1qPhpp5cxdSKuAckhFMQXZUtIfpvB2efS

These spreadsheets are used for the following exercises:
- **Sample – Superstore:** Exercises 1-6, 8-11, 16, 18, 22, 25-27, 29, 30 and 32
- **Global Superstore:** 7, 12-15, 17, 19, 20, 21, 23, 24, 28, 31 and 33-35

Chapter 1: Getting Started

Exercise 1: Logon to Tableau

Objective: This exercise will demonstrate how to launch Tableau and connect to an Excel spreadsheet data source

- Launch the **Windows Start Menu** which is displayed on Figure 1

Figure 1

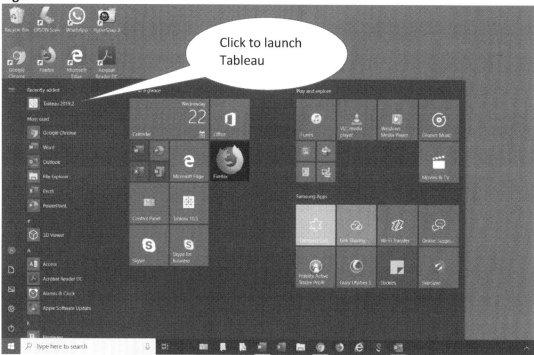

- Click **Tableau 2019.2** as shown on Figure 1, which will lead to the **Welcome** screen displayed on Figure 2

Figure 2

The left hand pane with the blue background, **Connect**, lists the various data sources that you can connect to. These sources include relational databases, online data sources, text files, as well as Excel. An Excel sheet is considered just like a database table. It is possible to join one or multiple tables (or sheets) in Tableau.

The middle section of the window with the light background, under **Open**, displays icons of workbooks that were used recently. In this case, no icon is displayed as this is a newly installed version of Tableau. Any workbook in this area can be launched by just clicking on it. The three items shown under **Sample Workbooks** are provided by Tableau and show up by default.

In our exercise, we will connect to an Excel spreadsheet. To connect:
- Click **Microsoft Excel** as shown on Figure 2, which will popup the window displayed on Figure 3

Figure 3

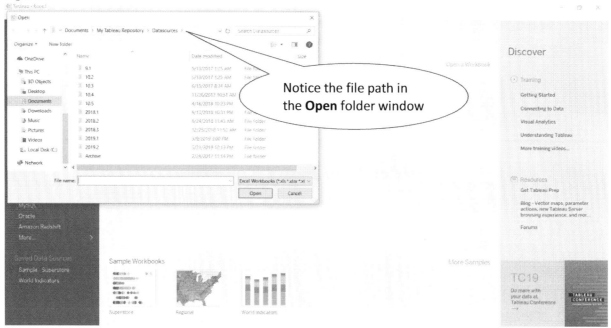

The file that we want to connect to is in a lower level folder. Therefore, we will need to drilldown into the folder structure until the desired file is displayed.

Navigate to the desired spreadsheet, **_Sample – Superstore_**, as follow:
- Documents > My Tableau Repository > Datasources > 2019.2 > en_US-US

When the drilldown has been completed, the display will be as shown on Figure 4.

Figure 4

On Figure 4, the **Sample – Superstore** spreadsheet is displayed.
- Click the **Sample – Superstore**, which will highlight it as shown on Figure 5

Figure 5

- Click the **Open** button as shown on Figure 5, which will open the **Sample – Superstore** spreadsheet and lead to the display on Figure 6

Figure 6

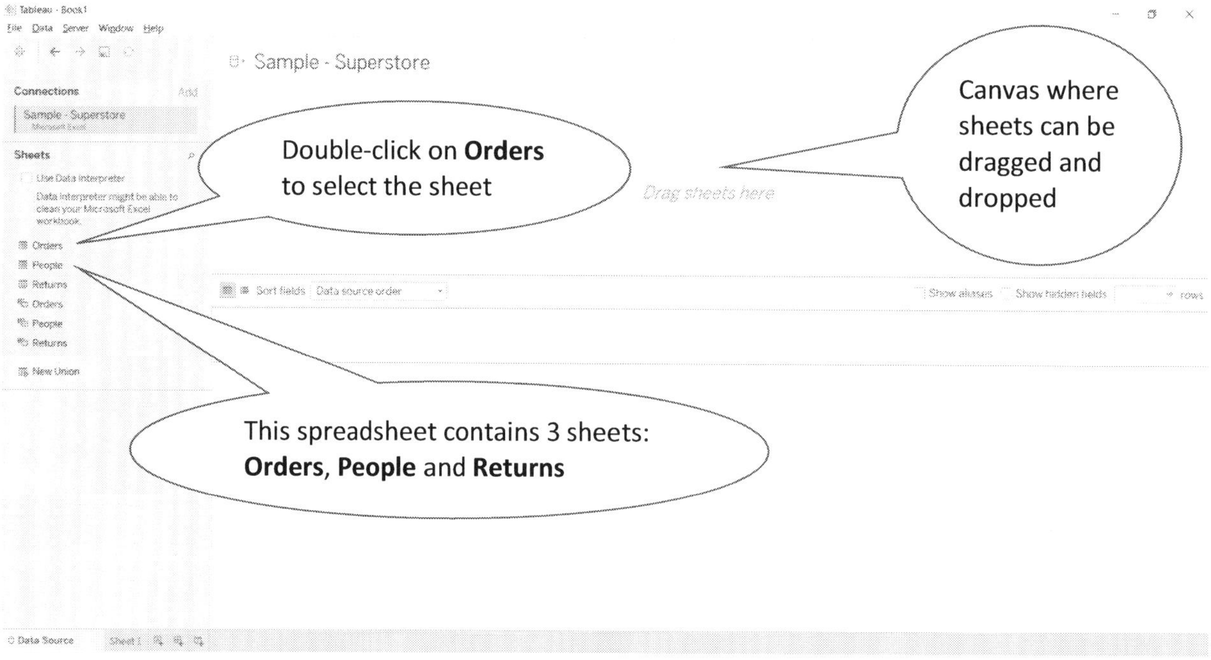

The **Sample - Superstore** spreadsheet contains three sheets: **Orders**, **People** and **Returns**. You can connect to one or more of the sheets or tables, such as **Orders**.

The **Orders** sheet can be opened for analysis using two methods:
1. Double-clicking on the **Orders** sheet
2. Dragging and dropping the **Orders** sheet onto the canvas

To drag and drop:
- Click the **Orders** sheet as shown on Figure 7

Figure 7

- Drag **Orders** onto the blank canvas area as shown on Figure 7, which will lead to the display on Figure 8

Figure 8

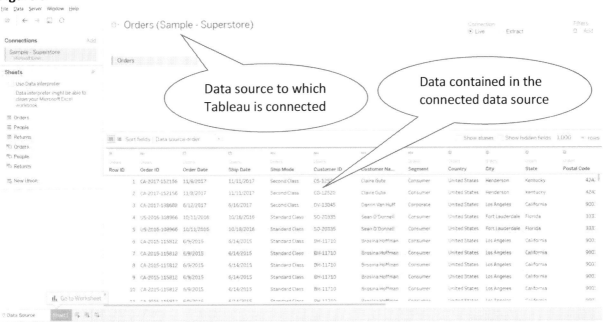

Figure 8 shows that the **Orders** sheet of the **Sample – Superstore** data source (Excel spreadsheet) is connected to Tableau. The lower section of the window shows the data which is contained in the selected sheet (**Orders**). The first row contains the column headers. The table itself contains sales data for customers buying specific products.

Exercise 2: Connect to Data Sources

Objective: This exercise will demonstrate how to connect to two data sources

Figure 1 shows the Tableau Welcome screen after the application is launched. The left-hand pane, under **Connect**, lists the various data sources to which Tableau can connect. These are split into three groups of data sources:
- To a file
- To a server
- Saved data sources

For this exercise as well as subsequent exercises, we will only use the first option—**To a file**. The other options can be used when we need to connect to other data sources which, in most cases, are databases.

Figure 1

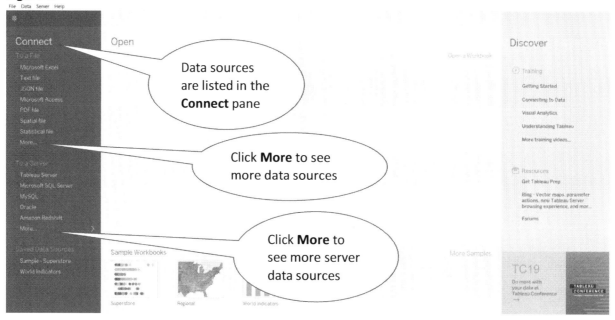

To display more data sources (files or servers):
- Click **More** under **To a Server** as shown on Figure 1, which will lead to Figure 2 where the additional data sources are listed

Figure 2

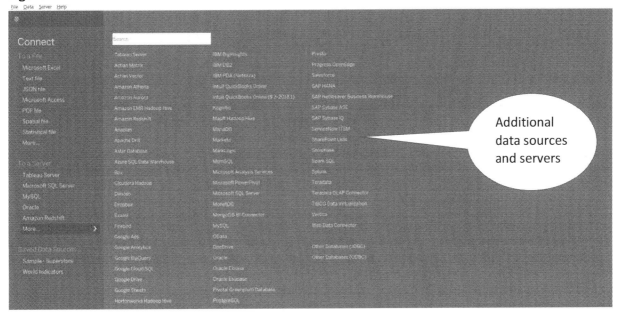

For this exercise, we will need the **Sample – Superstore** Excel spreadsheet data source. Now:

- Connect to the **Sample - Superstore** data source, using the method demonstrated in Exercise 1

If you want to, you can also connect directly to the **Sample – Superstore** Excel spreadsheet at the location where you downloaded it previously, which could be your desktop or another file folder.

To connect to the **Orders** sheet:

- Drag the **Orders** sheet onto the canvas as shown in Exercise 1, which will lead to Figure 3

Figure 3

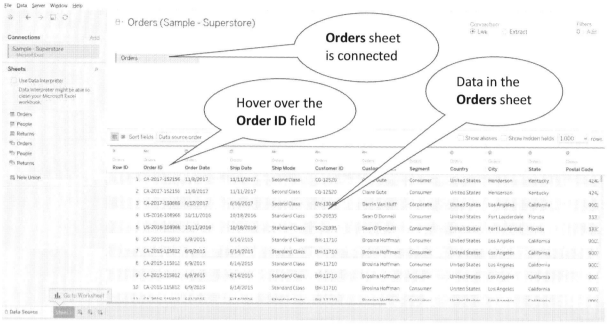

The source data can be used as-is. However, in some cases, data may need to be prepared so that it can enable better and/or easier analysis. For example, field names can be renamed so that they are easily understood by the business users. In some cases, a complex field may need to be split.

To rename the **Order ID** field:

- Hover over the **Order ID** field as shown on Figure 3, which will lead to Figure 4 (where the pulldown arrow is displayed above the field name)

Figure 4

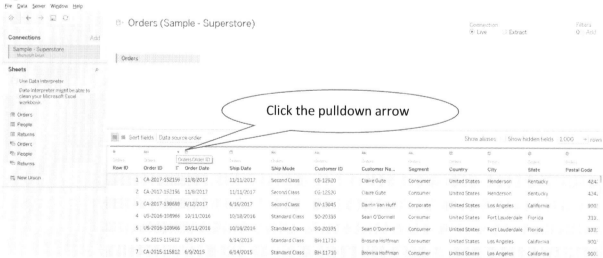

- Click the pulldown arrow for the **Order ID** field, which will popup the menu tree displayed on Figure 5

Figure 5

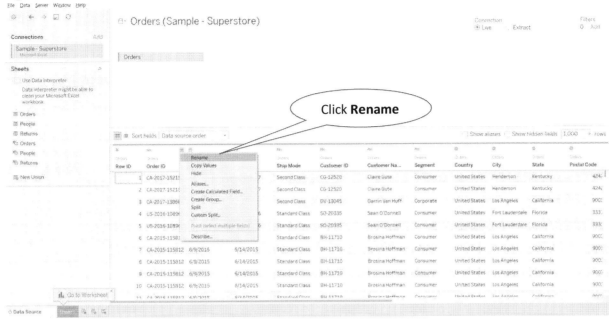

- Click **Rename** as shown on Figure 5, which will lead to Figure 6

Figure 6

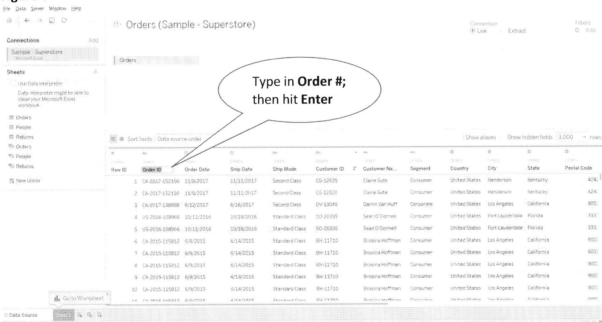

Notice that the **Order ID** field name can now be edited. To edit the field name:
- Type in the new field name (**Order #**) as shown on Figure 6
- Hit **Enter**, which will rename the field and lead to the display on Figure 7

Figure 7

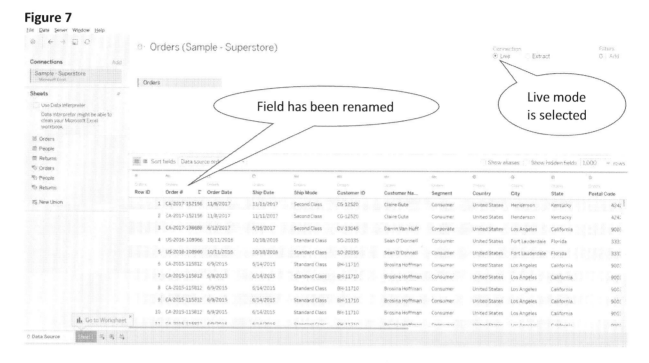

There are two ways in which data can be accessed and used by Tableau: Live and Extract. In **Connect Live**, a direct connection is made with the data source. In this mode, if the source data changes, it is immediately reflected in the visualizations and any analysis being performed. In the **Extract** mode, data is pulled into the Tableau data engine, which takes the data offline. No live connection is maintained with the source system (from which the querying load is offloaded). In the extract mode, however, analysis can only be performed upto the time when the extract was pulled. When real-time data needs to be analyzed, this option will not work.

On Figure 7, **Live** mode is currently selected. In the next step, we will switch from the **Live** mode to the **Extract** mode. We will start with Figure 8, where **Live** mode is selected.

Figure 8

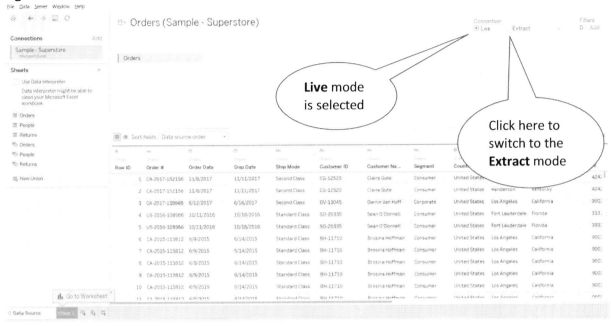

- Click the **Extract** radio button, as shown on Figure 8, to switch to the **Extract** mode which will lead to Figure 9

Figure 9

To display the Worksheet:
- Click the Worksheet tab (**Sheet 1**) as shown on Figure 9, which will lead to the worksheet displayed on Figure 10

Figure 10

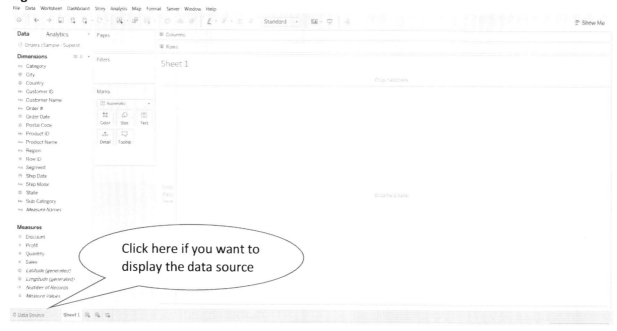

You can toggle between a worksheet and its data source. If you are working on a worksheet and need to go back to the data source:

- Click the **Data Source** tab as shown on Figure 10, which will open the data source window

Additional data sources can be added to an existing data source. Figure 11 shows three data sources: **Orders**, **People**, and **Returns**. Orders has already been connected. Notice that the connection is live.

Figure 11

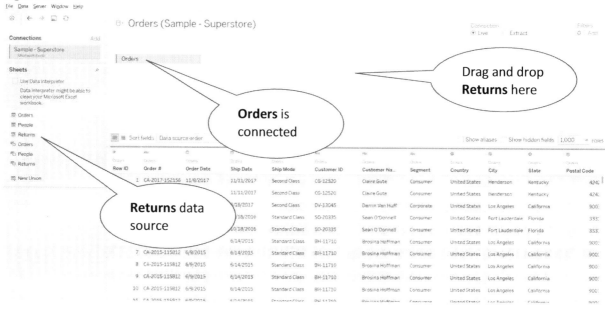

To add the second data source, **Returns:**

- Drag and drop the **Returns** sheet onto the canvas next to **Orders** as shown on Figure 11, which will lead to Figure 12

Figure 12

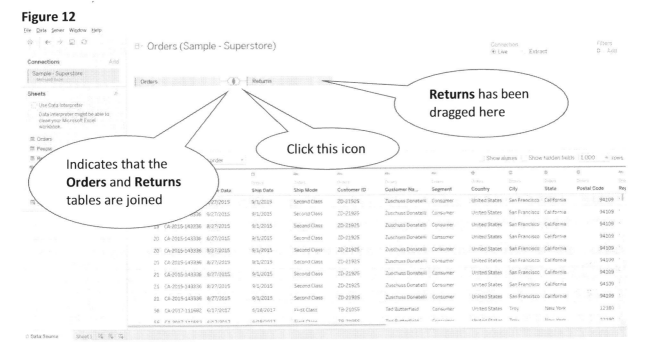

Tableau automatically joined the two tables, **Orders** and **Returns**, as an inner join.

- Click the **Join** icon as shown on Figure 12, which will display the join details on Figure 13

Figure 13

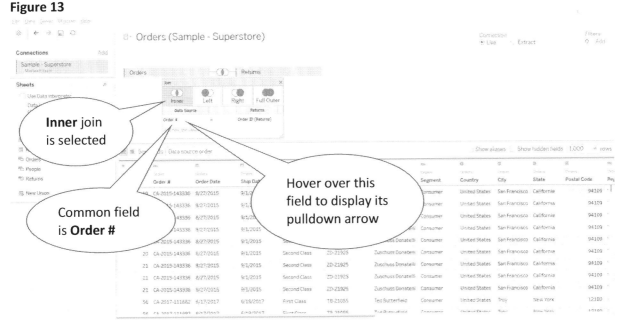

Tableau automatically determined that **Order #** is a common field for the two tables, **Orders** and **Returns**, as shown on Figure 13. It also provides the option to select a different field to join two tables.

To use a different field for joining the two tables:
- Hover over the **Order #** field as shown on Figure 13, which will display its pulldown arrow shown on Figure 14

Figure 14

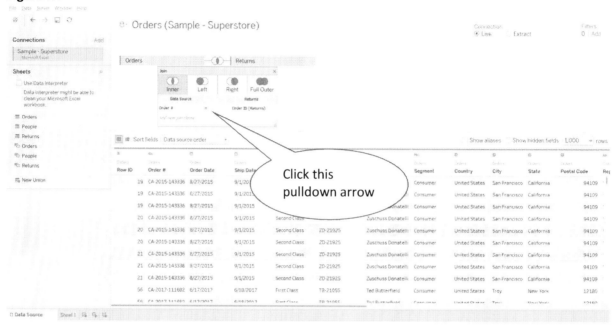

To use a different field for joining the two tables:
- Click the **Order #** pulldown arrow as shown on Figure 14, which will lead to Figure 15

Figure 15

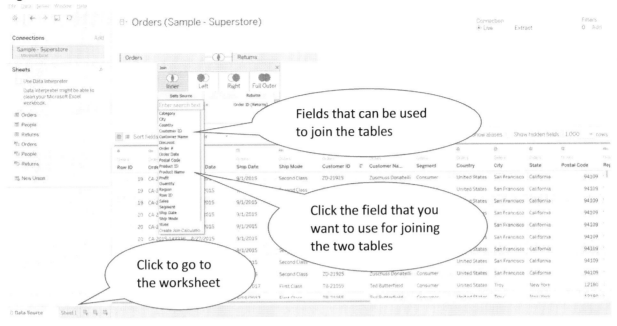

To select a different field to join the two tables:
- Click the desired field from the list displayed on Figure 15, which will change the join to the field that is clicked (instead of **Order #**)

We will now see how the worksheet changed after the second data source (**Returns**) was added:
- Click the **Sheet 1** tab as shown on Figure 15, which will lead to Figure 16

Figure 16

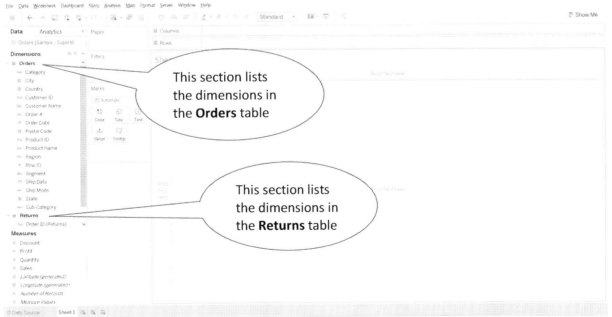

On Figure 16, the dimensions for the **Orders** table as well as the **Returns** table are displayed. You can use the pane's scrollbar to display additional **Returns** dimensions, which are currently hidden.

You can search for a field, which is a useful feature when a table has too many dimensions or measures. Figure 17 shows a worksheet with many dimensions—some currently displayed while others can only be displayed after scrolling.

Figure 17

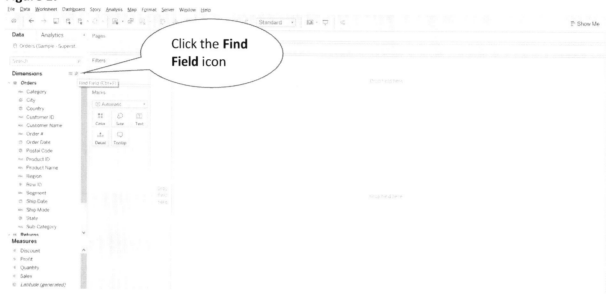

To search for a dimension:

- Click the **Find Field** icon shown on Figure 17, which will lead to Figure 18, where the search box is displayed (with the **Search** prompt)

Figure 18

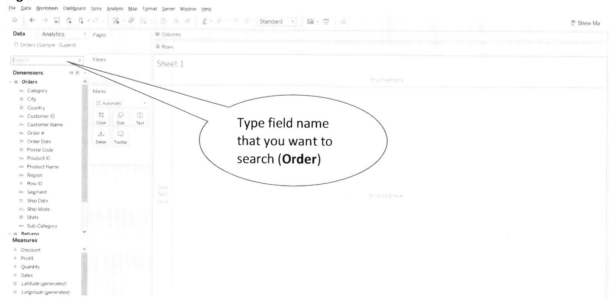

To search for the key word **Order**:

- Type **Order** in the search box as shown on Figure 18, which will highlight the field(s) matching the search criteria as shown on Figure 19

Figure 19

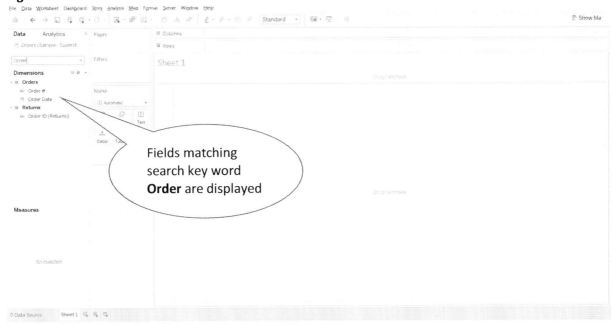

Exercise 3: Tableau Interface and Navigation

Objective: This exercise will provide an overview of the Tableau workbook interface

Note that this exercise does not require any hands-on activity—it just provides an overview of the Tableau interface.

After connecting to a data source, you will see a blank sheet as displayed on Figure 1, where data visualizations can be developed. Through the Tableau interface shown on Figure 1 and Figure 2, many powerful and useful features can be accessed.

Figure 1

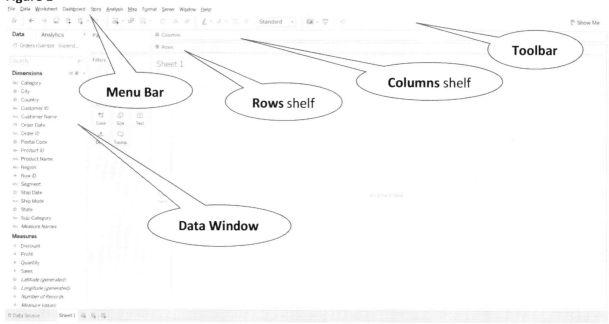

On Figure 1, the **Menu Bar** at the top of the window provides access to many powerful features. Below it is the **Toolbar**, which contains many buttons such as **Undo, Redo, Save**, **New Data Source, New Worksheet, Duplicate, Swap, Sort, etc.** These buttons are contextual and, therefore, only the relevant ones are highlighted—based on the current state of the worksheet.

The Tableau window is divided into shelves, which are sometimes referred to as **Cards**. The shelves are:
- Columns Shelf
- Rows Shelf
- Filter Shelf
- Pages Shelf

As highlighted on Figure 2, the **Marks Card** contains additional shelves on which fields can be placed directly (through drag and drop). Mark card shelves include **Color, Size, Text, Detail and Tooltip**. Clicking on these shelves activate popup boxes which enable their characteristics, such as labels, to be edited.

The default **Marks** type is **Automatic**, which is the selection shown in Figure 2. However, there are many Mark types which can be used instead of the default (Automatic).

Figure 2

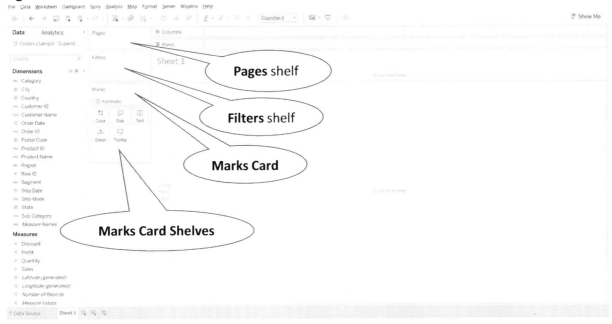

The **Data Window** contains two tabs, **Data** and **Analytics**, which are highlighted on Figure 3.

Figure 3

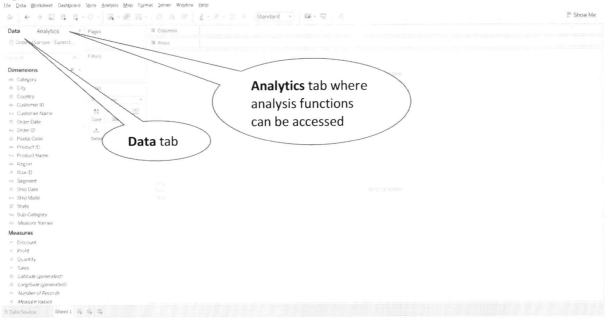

The default tab is **Data** which displays the dimensions and measures used to develop visualizations. The **Analytics** tab displays a completely different set of options that are focused on analysis.

Figure 4

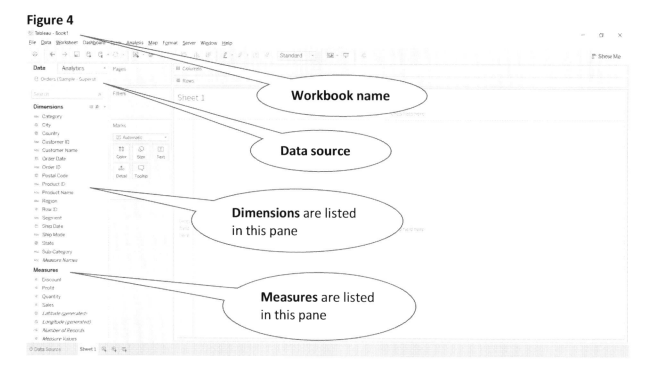

On Figure 4, the data source currently connected, **Orders (Sample – Superstore)**, is displayed at the top of the data window. Views (visualizations) are built by dragging and dropping fields from the **Data Window** onto the canvas or directly onto the shelves.

Figure 5 shows the menu tree which is displayed when the **File** option is selected on the **Menu Bar**.

Figure 5

Figure 6 shows the menu tree which is displayed when the **Data** option is selected on the **Menu Bar**.

Figure 6

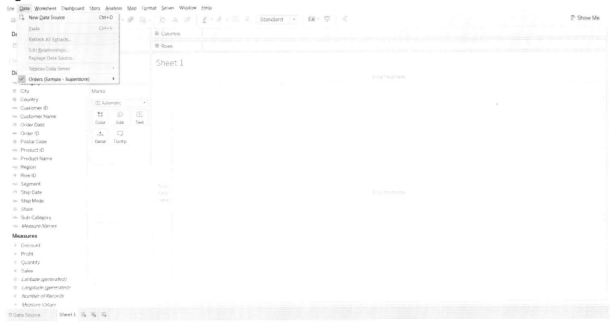

Figure 7 shows the menu tree which is displayed when the **Worksheet** option is selected on the **Menu Bar**.

Figure 7

Figure 8 shows the menu tree which is displayed when the **Dashboard** option is selected on the **Menu Bar**.

Figure 8

Figure 9 shows the menu tree which is displayed when the **Analysis** option is selected on the **Menu Bar**.

Figure 9

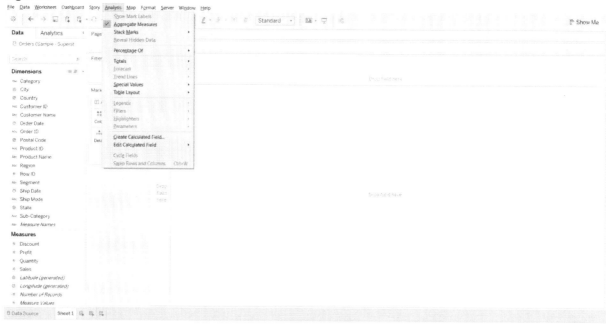

Figure 10 shows the menu tree which is displayed when the **Format** option is selected on the **Menu Bar**.

Figure 10

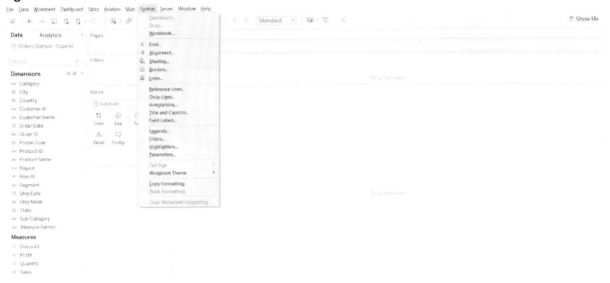

Note that:
- Tableau does not save a worksheet automatically; hence, you must save your work before exiting
- Buttons are contextual; hence, the functions available depend on what is going on in the sheet

To undo or reverse an action, use the **Back** arrow. The **Back** and **Forward** arrows, highlighted on Figure 11, can be used to navigate and go back/forward as visualizations are developed and/or modified.

Figure 11

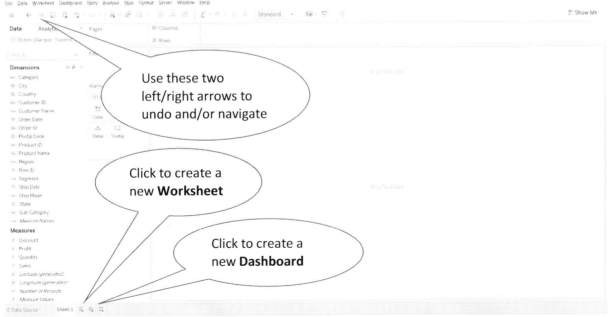

The **Sheet** tabs at the bottom of the window, highlighted on Figure 11, are used to create new worksheets, dashboards and stories. Sheets can be moved around (by dragging), renamed, and duplicated. By right-clicking on the appropriate sheet, a menu tree will popup which can enable:

- Copying a sheet
- Renaming a sheet
- Deleting a sheet
- Exporting a sheet
- Creating a new worksheet, dashboard or story

To create a new worksheet or a new dashboard:

- Click the New Worksheet icon as shown on Figure 11
- Click the New Dashboard icon as shown on Figure 11

The layout displayed for a **Dashboard** is different compared to a **Worksheet**. Figures 1 through 11 displayed worksheet layouts. Figure 12 displays the layout when a dashboard is created.

Figure 12

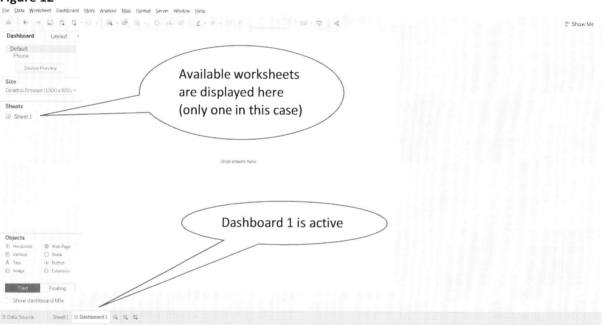

When a dashboard window is active:

- Data Window (used in Worksheets) is replaced by the Dashboard Window
- It lists all the sheets available (in the left-hand window)
- It lists the Dashboard objects
- Display the controls for the objects
- Displays the sizing options

If two data sources are used in a worksheet, they will be displayed in the **Data Window** as shown on Figure 13, where the data sources are:

- Sample – Superstore
- Global Superstore

Figure 13

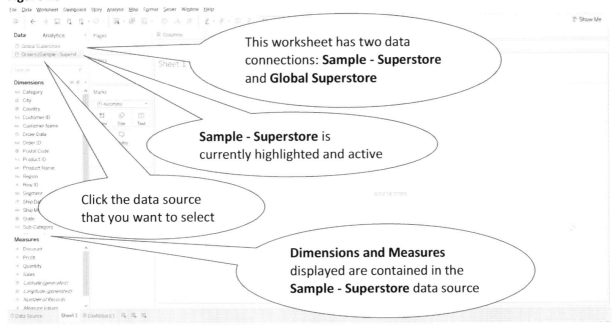

The view displayed in the **Data Window** on the left-hand side, which is a list of dimensions and measures, depends on the data source that is selected. On Figure 13, the dimensions and measures displayed belong to the highlighted **Sample - Superstore** data source.

To display the dimensions and measures for the **Global Superstore**, click on it which will change the view as shown on Figure 14, where the **Global Superstore's** dimensions and measures are displayed.

Figure 14

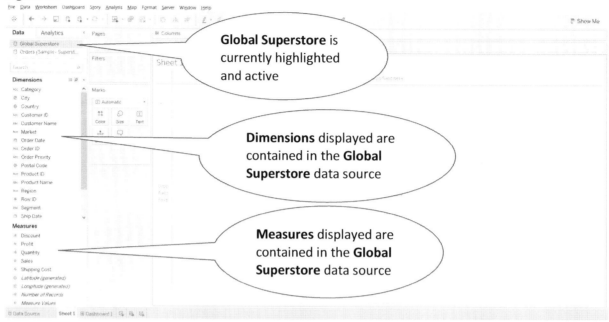

While most fields are common in both data sources, the **Shipping Cost** measure is only displayed in the **Global Superstore**, as shown in Figure 14.

Exercise 4: Develop a Simple Visualization

Objective: This exercise will demonstrate how to develop a simple visualization

To start this exercise:
- Launch Tableau
- Connect to the **Sample - Superstore** Excel file, using the procedure demonstrated in Exercise 1, which will lead to Figure 1

Figure 1

- Click the **Sheet 1** tab as shown on Figure 1, which will lead to Figure 2 where reports and visualizations can be developed

Figure 2

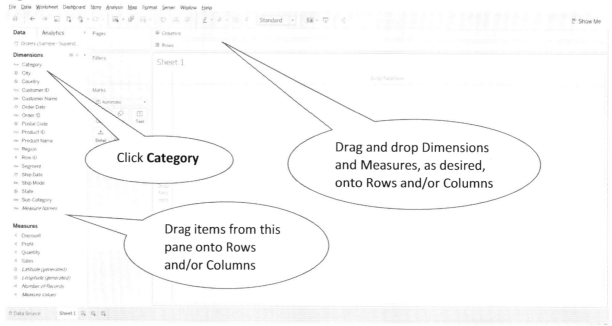

The left-hand side of Figure 2 shows two groups:
- Dimensions
- Measures

Dimensions are fields such as product, region, and customer. They are used to slice and dice the data to provide different perspectives. Dimensions are color coded blue in the data pane and in the view.

Measures are metrics, i.e., the numbers, used for analysis. They are color coded green.

In the following steps, we will drag and drop the desired dimensions and measures onto the Columns and Rows.

- Click **Category** as shown on Figure 2, which will lead to Figure 3 (where **Category** is highlighted)

Figure 3

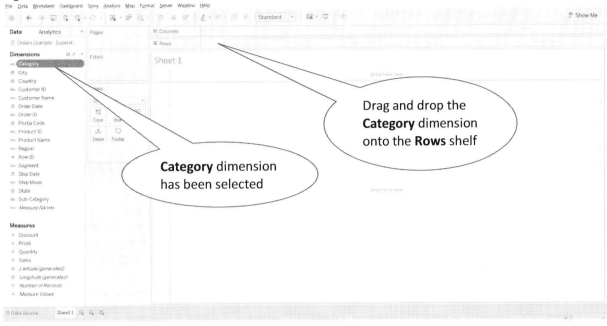

- Drag and drop **Category** onto the **Row** shelf as shown on Figure 3, which will lead to Figure 4

Figure 4

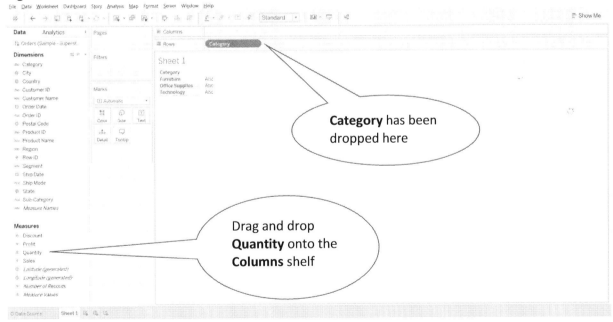

- Drag and drop **Quantity** onto the **Columns** shelf as shown on Figure 4, which will lead to Figure 5

Figure 5

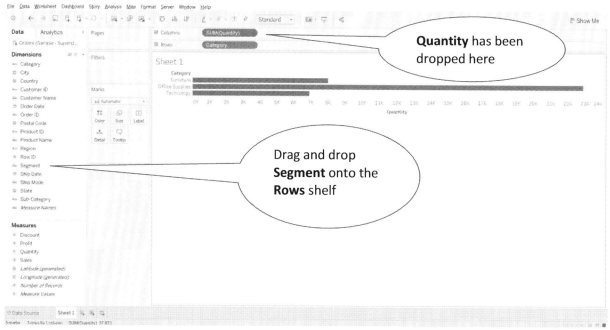

Quantity has been dropped here

Drag and drop **Segment** onto the **Rows** shelf

- Drag and drop **Segment** onto the **Rows** shelf as shown on Figure 5, which will lead to Figure 6

Figure 6

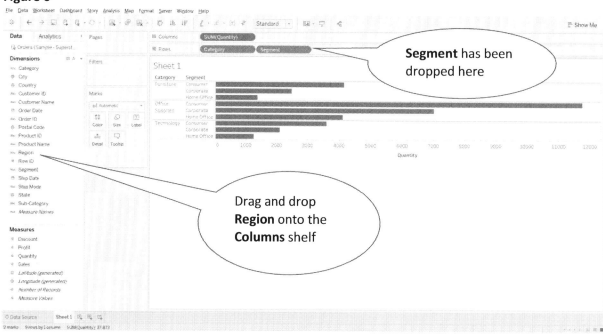

Segment has been dropped here

Drag and drop **Region** onto the **Columns** shelf

- Drag and drop **Region** onto the **Columns** shelf as shown on Figure 6, which will lead to Figure 7

Figure 7

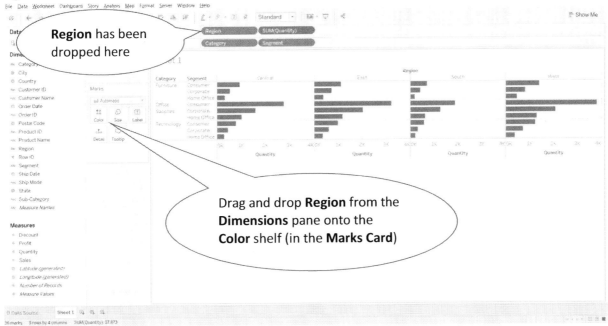

To enhance the display by utilizing color:

- Drag and drop **Region** from the Dimensions pane onto the **Color** shelf (on the **Marks Card**), as shown on Figure 7 which will lead to Figure 8

Figure 8

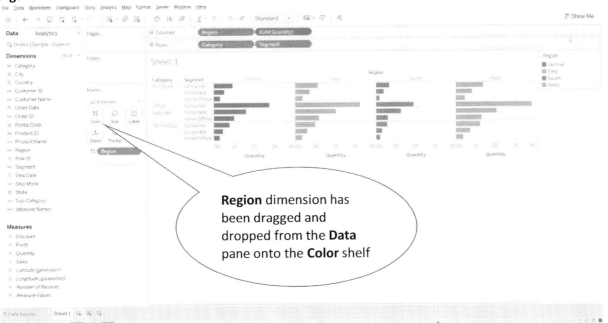

Exercise 5: Save a Workbook

Objective: This exercise will demonstrate how to save a Tableau Workbook (.twb) as well as a Tableau Packaged Workbook (.twbx)

Tableau provides two options to save a workbook. In the first option, only the workbook is saved (as a .twb file). In the second option, the data associated with the workbook is packaged and saved (as a .twbx file). We will start with Figure 1, which displays a view based on Category, Region and Sales.

Figure 1

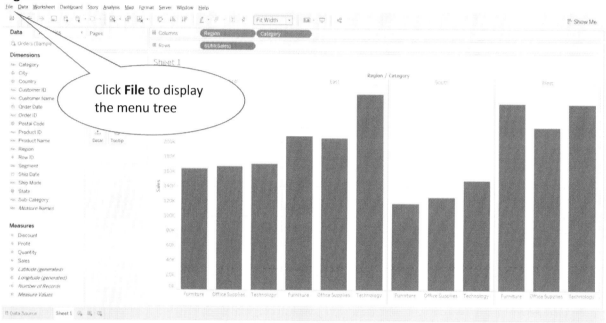

- Click **File** on the **Menu Bar** as shown on Figure 1, which will popup the menu tree displayed on Figure 2

Figure 2

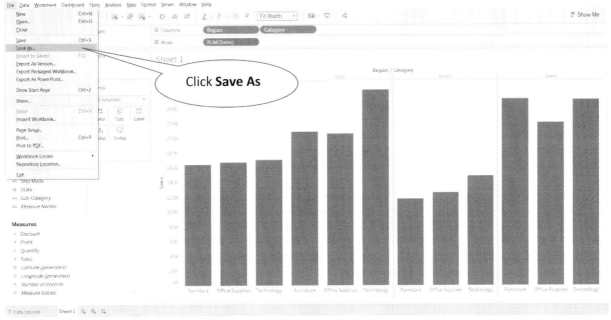

- Click the **Save As** menu tree item as shown on Figure 2, which will lead to the popup **Save As** window displayed on Figure 3

Selecting the **Save As** option will enable you to rename the default file name which is provided by the system. It will also provide an option to select the file type.

Figure 3

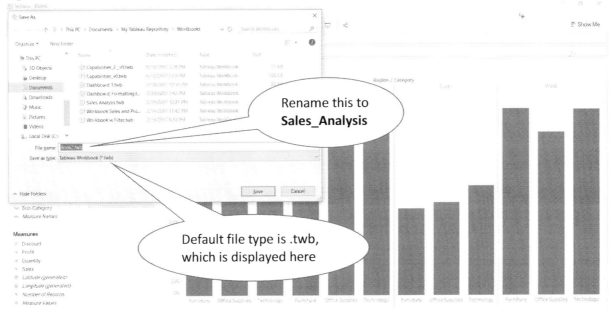

Rename this to
Sales_Analysis

Default file type is .twb, which is displayed here

We will now rename the Tableau generated default file name which, in this case, is **Book2**.
- Type in **Sales_Analysis** as shown on Figure 3, which will lead to the display on Figure 4

Figure 4

- Click **Save** as shown on Figure 4, which will save the workbook as **Sales_Analysis.twb** and lead to Figure 5

Figure 5

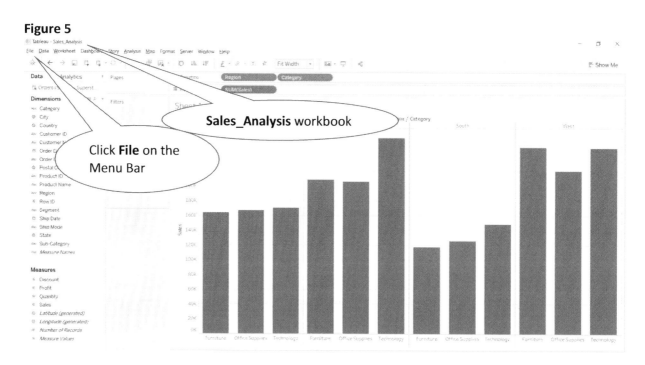

We will now show how a workbook can be saved with its associated data as a .twbx file.

- Click **File** on the **Menu Bar** as shown on Figure 5, which will lead to the menu tree displayed on Figure 6

Figure 6

- Click the **Export Packaged Workbook** menu tree item as shown on Figure 6, which will popup the **Export Packaged Workbook** window displayed on Figure 7

Figure 7

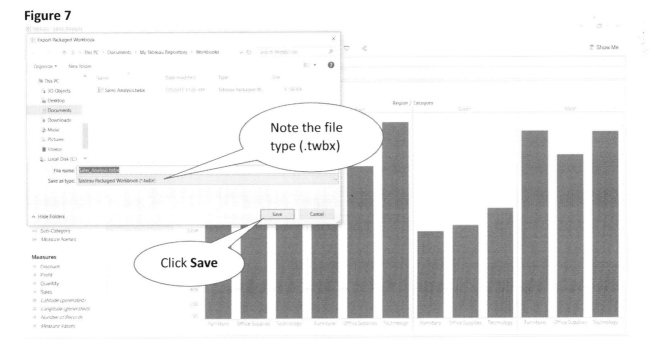

- Navigate to the folder where the workbook is to be saved (or accept the default location)
- Click **Save** as shown on Figure 7, which will save the Packaged Workbook (.twbx) and lead to Figure 8

When a file is saved with the .twbx extension, it embeds the data in the workbook. This is useful when you want to share it with another user. When the recipient opens the .twbx file, it contains the workbook and the associated data and, hence, can be used without connecting to the data source (which may or may not be available to that user).

Figure 8

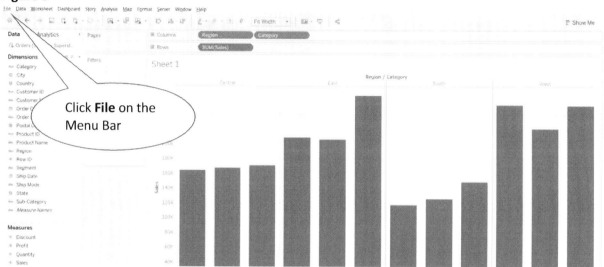

- Click **File** on the **Menu Bar** as shown on Figure 8, which will display the menu tree on Figure 9

Figure 9

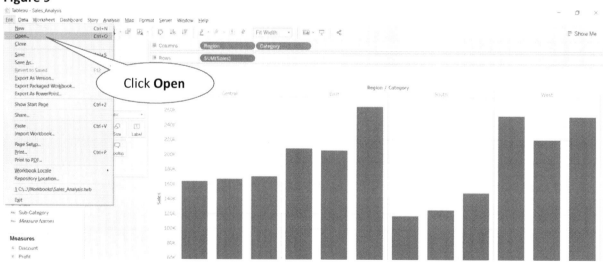

- Click the **Open** menu tree item as shown on Figure 9, which will lead to the **Open** popup window displayed on Figure 10

Figure 10

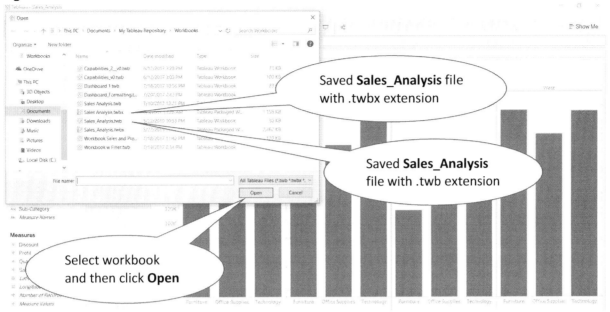

The **Open** popup window displays two files that were saved in this exercise:
- Tableau Workbook (without the data—has .twb file extension)
- Tableau Packaged Workbook (with embedded data—has .twbx file extension)

To open a saved workbook:
- Click the desired file in the **Open** window
- Click **Open** as shown on Figure 10, which will open the selected workbook

Note that there are multiple ways to execute a function in Tableau. A workbook can also be saved with a .twbx extension through the **Save As** menu tree item by executing the following steps:
- Click **File** on the Menu Bar
- Navigate via *File > Save As*, which will lead to Figure 11

Figure 11

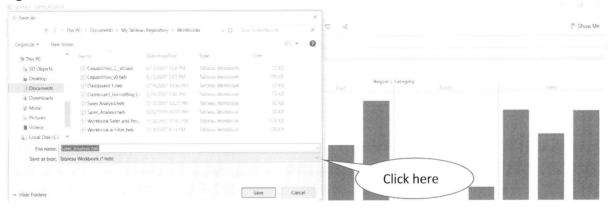

Note that the default selection for the **Save as type** is *Tableau Workbook (*.twb)* as shown in Figure 11.

- Click the pulldown arrow for *Save as type* as shown on Figure 11, which will lead to Figure 12

Figure 12

- Select the option **Tableau Packaged Workbook (*.twbx)**
- Click **Save** to save the workbook with the .twbx extension

Exercise 6: Copy and Delete Worksheets

Objective: This exercise will demonstrate how to copy or delete a worksheet

We will start with the **Sales by Region and Category** worksheet displayed on Figure 1.

Figure 1

To make a duplicate copy of the worksheet:
- Right-click **Sheet 1** as shown on Figure 1, which will popup the menu tree displayed on Figure 2

Figure 2

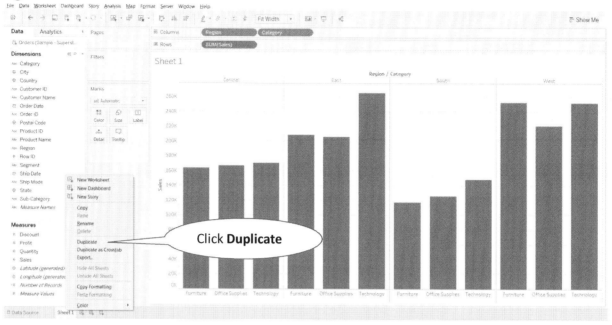

- Click the **Duplicate** menu tree item as shown on Figure 2, which will lead to Figure 3

Figure 3

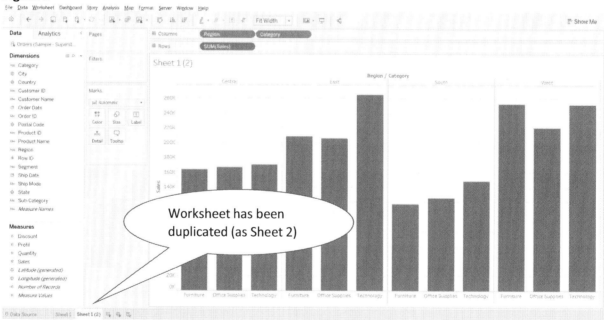

Figure 3 now shows two worksheets:
- **Sheet 1** (original)
- **Sheet 1 (2)** (duplicate of Sheet 1)

To delete a worksheet:

- Right-click on the sheet to be deleted, **Sheet 1 (2)**, which will popup the menu tree displayed on Figure 4

Figure 4

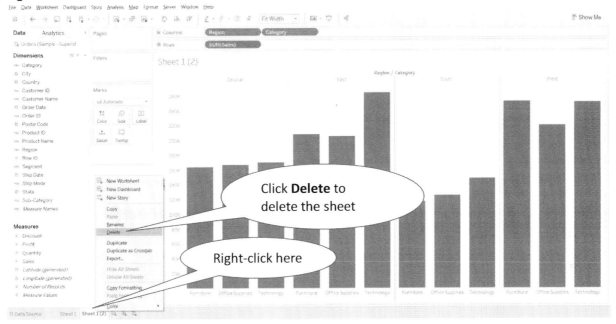

- Click the **Delete** menu tree item as shown on Figure 4, which will delete **Sheet 1 (2)**

Chapter 2: Customization

Exercise 7: Add, Delete and Rename Dimensions

Objective: This exercise demonstrates how a dimension or measure can be added or removed from a visualization and, also, how to rename a dimension

Note: Use the **Global Superstore** file for this exercise

Start with Figure 1, which includes one dimension (**Region**) and one measure (**Sales**).

Figure 1

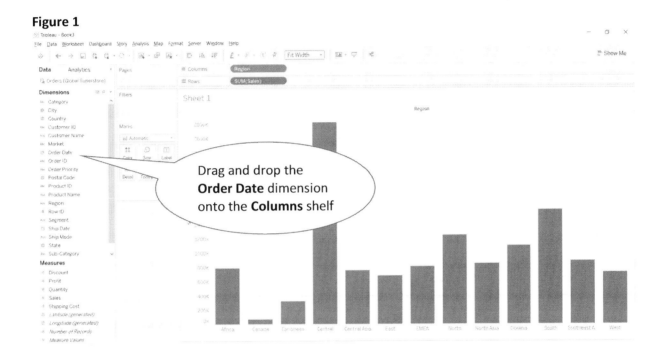

To add the **Order Date** dimension:
- Drag and drop **Order Date** from the **Data Window** onto the **Columns** shelf as shown on Figure 1, which will lead to Figure 2

Figure 2

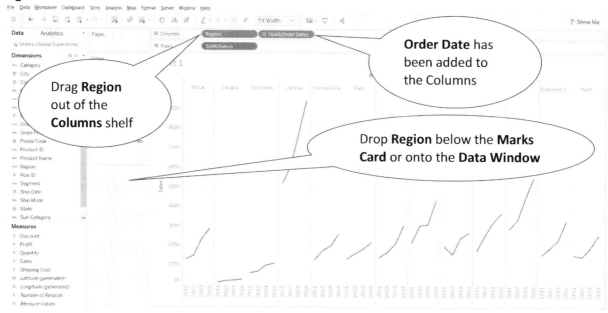

To remove the **Region** dimension:

- Drag and drop **Region** from the **Columns** shelf onto the **Data Window** or below the **Marks Card**, as shown on Figure 2, which will lead to Figure 3

Figure 3

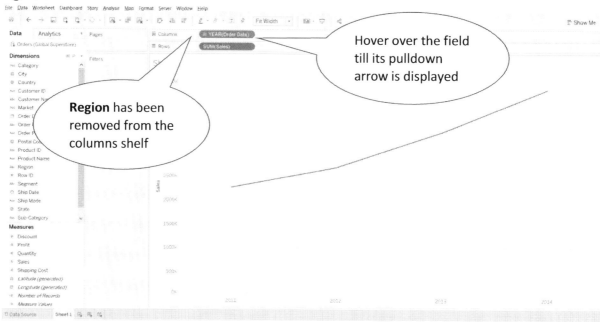

An alternative method can be used to remove a dimension, which is described in the next step.

To remove **Year** from the columns shelf:
- Hover over **YEAR(Order Date)** as shown on Figure 3
- Click on the pulldown menu when it is displayed, which will lead to Figure 4 where a menu tree is displayed

Figure 4

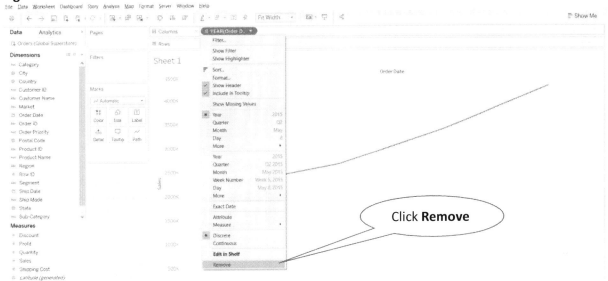

- Click **Remove** as shown on Figure 4, which will remove the dimension

The procedure to add and/or delete a measure is similar to the one used to add/delete a dimension, which was demonstrated earlier in this exercise.

Sometimes, the dimensions and measures in the source files have names that are not clear to the end users. Therefore, renaming them can make the system less confusing and more user-friendly. Tableau provides the ability to rename dimensions and measures in the **Data Window**, where they are displayed.

We will now rename the **Postal Code** dimension displayed on Figure 5 (which is a new blank worksheet).

Figure 5

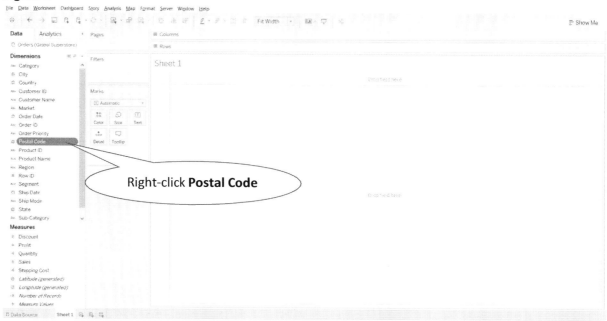

To rename the **Postal Code** dimension:

• Right-click **Postal Code** as shown on Figure 5, which will popup the menu tree shown on Figure 6

Figure 6

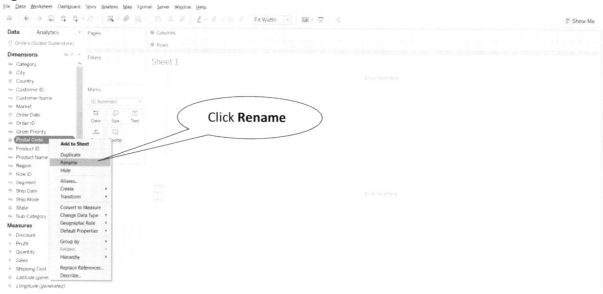

• Click **Rename** as shown on Figure 6, which will lead to Figure 7 where the **Postal Code** field can be edited

Figure 7

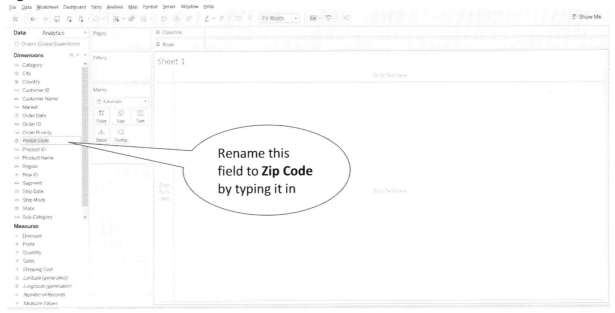

- Rename the highlighted field name from **Postal Code** to **Zip Code**, by typing in **Zip Code** as shown on Figure 7, which will lead to Figure 8

Figure 8

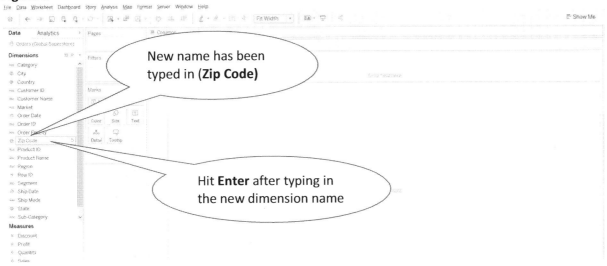

After the new name has been typed in:
- Hit **Enter**, which will lead to Figure 9 where the new name is displayed

Figure 9

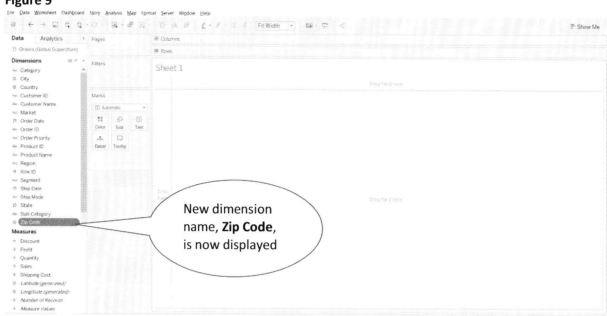

New dimension name, **Zip Code**, is now displayed

Exercise 8: Show Me Window

Objective: This exercise will demonstrate how to use the **Show Me** tool for selecting the appropriate visualization for the data being analyzed

Show Me is a powerful tool that helps users pick the appropriate view for the data being analyzed. The **Show Me** window contains commonly used chart types, which can help a user to get started with visual analysis. Based on the data that is being analyzed, the **Show Me** tool highlights only the relevant views that can be developed, while the others are greyed out.

Figure 1 shows a blank worksheet, where the **Show Me** window is minimized.

Figure 1

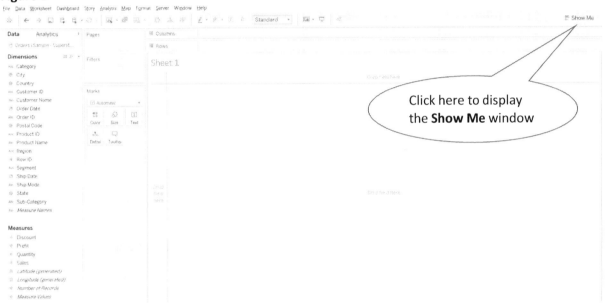

To display the **Show Me** window:
- Click the **Show Me** button as shown on Figure 1, which will lead to the display on Figure 2

Figure 2

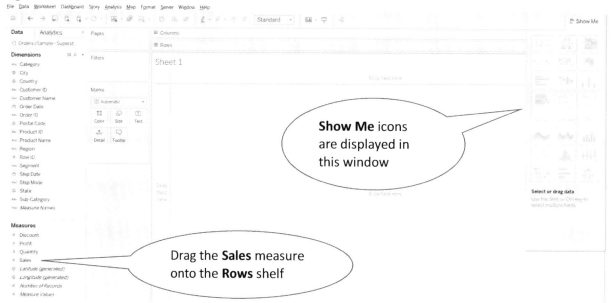

- Drag the **Sales** measure onto the **Rows** shelf as shown on Figure 2, which will lead to the chart displayed on Figure 3

Figure 3

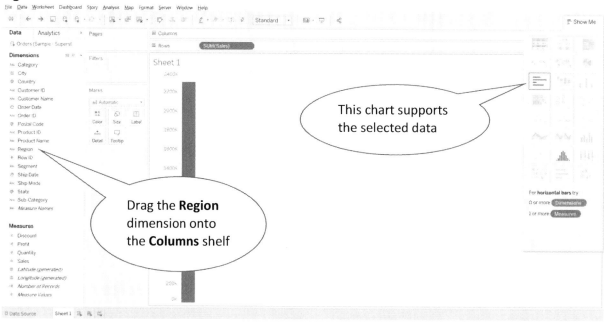

- Drag the **Region** dimension onto the **Columns** shelf as shown on Figure 3, which will lead to the chart displayed on Figure 4

Figure 4

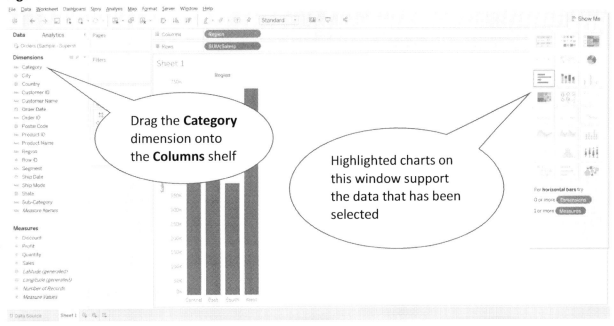

- Drag the **Category** dimension onto the **Columns** shelf as shown on Figure 4, which will lead to the chart displayed on Figure 5

Figure 5

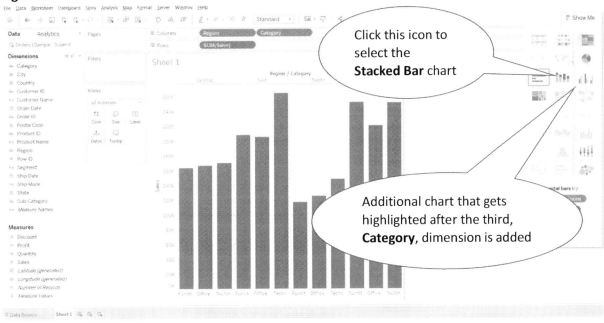

We will now use the **Show Me** window to change the type of visualization that is displayed. Clicking on any highlighted icon in the **Show Me** window will display the selected visualization.

To select the stacked bar chart:

- Click the **Stacked Bar** icon in the **Show Me** window as shown on Figure 5, which will lead to the visualization displayed on Figure 6

Figure 6

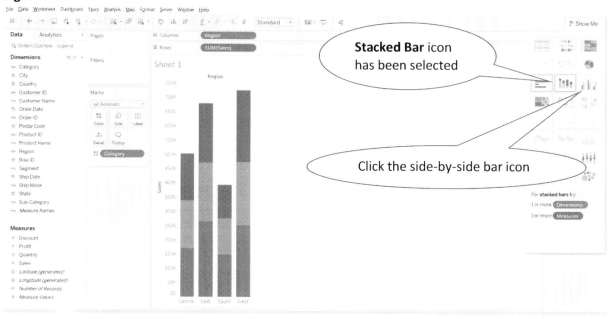

To select the side-by-side bars:

- Click the **Side-by-Side bar** icon in the **Show Me** window as shown on Figure 6, which will lead to the visualization displayed on Figure 7

Figure 7

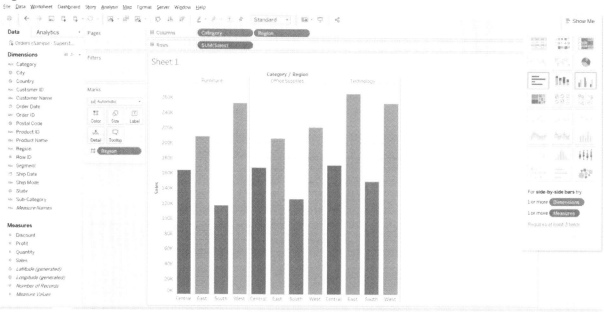

If you want to see which visualizations can be developed without dragging the dimensions and measures onto the **Columns Shelf** and the **Rows Shelf**, use the following steps (which select multiple items in one step):

- Open a new Worksheet (like Figure 1)
- Click the 1st measure (**Sales**)

While holding down the **CTRL** key:

- Click the 1st dimension (**Region**); On a Mac, use Apple + Click
- Click the 2nd dimension (**Category**); On a Mac, use Apple + Click

This will highlight, on the **Show Me** window, all the visualizations that can be developed when these three items are selected, as shown in Figure 8.

Figure 8

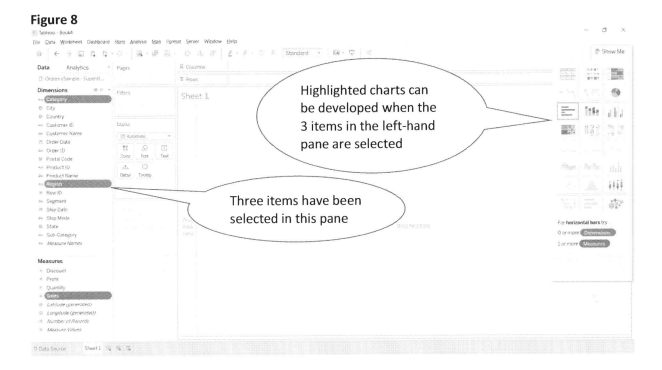

63

Exercise 9: Chart Types

Objective: This exercise will demonstrate how to change the display from one chart type to another

Figure 1 shows a bar chart for the sum of Sales by Region and Category.

Figure 1

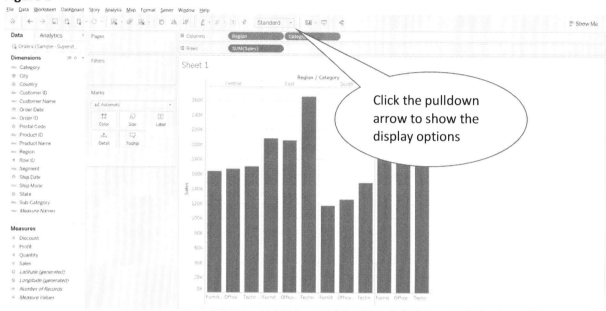

To make the chart more readable, utilize the white (blank) space to the right of the bars:
- Click the pulldown arrow shown on Figure 1, which will lead to Figure 2 where the menu tree is displayed

Figure 2

- Click the **Fit Width** menu tree item as shown on Figure 2, which will lead to Figure 3 where the white space has been eliminated

Figure 3

Figure 3 displays the **Show Me** button which can be used to:
- Suggest the appropriate chart based on the selected data or
- Change the type of chart that is displayed

While **Show Me** displays many chart types, it only highlights the ones that can be used with the underlying data. If a chart cannot be used, it is not highlighted.

To change the displayed chart type:
- Click the **Show Me** button as shown on Figure 3, which will lead to Figure 4 where the various chart types are displayed

Figure 4

On the **Show Me** window on Figure 4, only the highlighted charts can be used. They support the underlying data and, hence, are highlighted while the remaining ones are subdued. One of the chart types highlighted on Figure 4 is the stacked bar chart.

- Click the **Stacked Bar** chart icon as shown on Figure 4, which will lead to the display on Figure 5

Figure 5

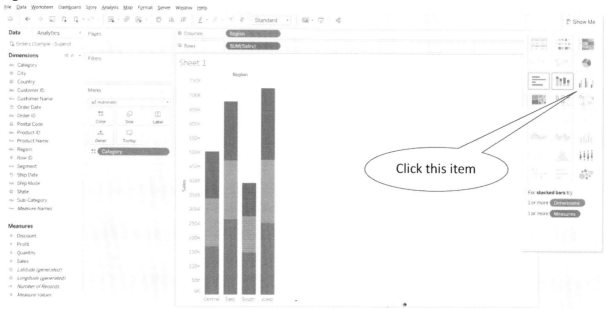

To change the chart type, all you will need to do is click on the desired chart in the **Show Me** window:
- Click the chart icon as shown on Figure 5, which will lead to the chart displayed on Figure 6

66

Figure 6

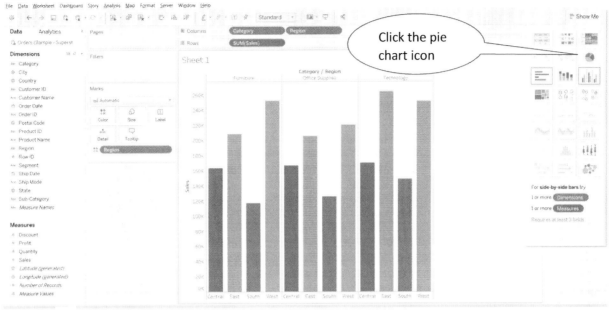

To display the data as a pie chart:
- Click the pie chart icon as shown on Figure 6, which will lead to the display on Figure 7

Figure 7

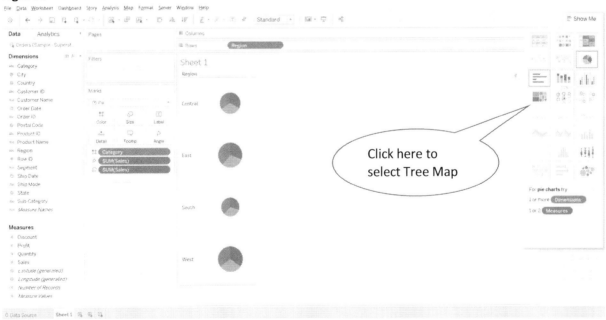

To display the data as a Tree Map:
- Click the Tree Map icon as shown on Figure 7, which will lead to the display on Figure 8

Figure 8

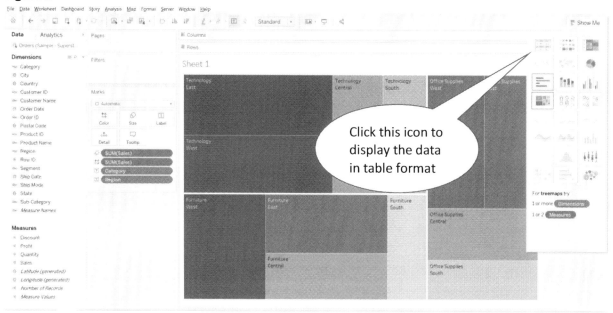

Click this icon to display the data in table format

To display the data in table format:

- Click the **Text Table** icon as shown on Figure 8, which will lead to Figure 9 where the data is displayed in a table format

Figure 9

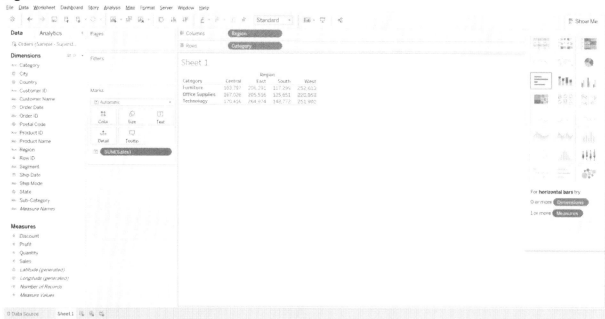

Chapter 3: Analysis

Exercise 10: Basic Analysis

Objective: This exercise will demonstrate some basic analysis functions in Tableau

To start this exercise:
- Launch Tableau
- Connect to the **Orders** sheet in the **Sample – Superstore** Excel file, as shown on Figure 1

Figure 1

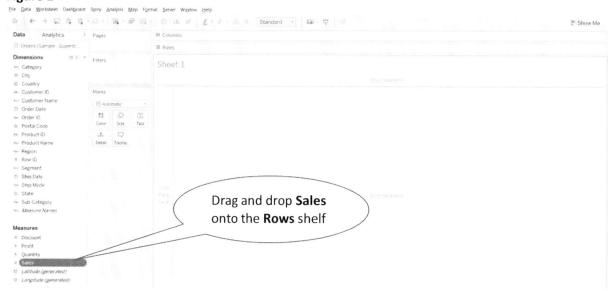

- Drag and drop the **Sales** measure onto the **Rows** shelf as shown on Figure 1, which will lead to Figure 2

Figure 2

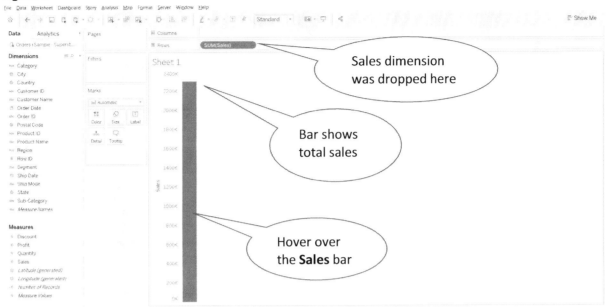

- Hover over the **Sales** bar as shown on Figure 2, which will display the total sales figure as shown on Figure 3 ($2,297,201)

Figure 3

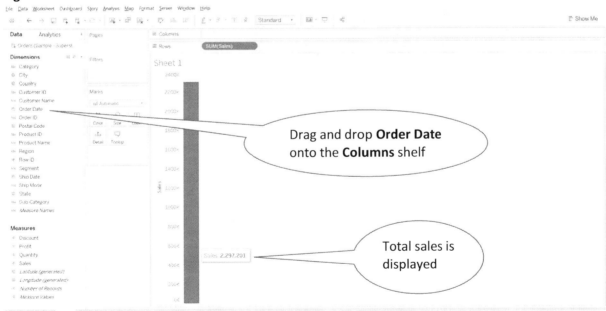

To view the results over time:

- Drag and drop **Order Date** onto the **Columns** shelf as shown on Figure 3, which will lead to the display shown on Figure 4

Figure 4

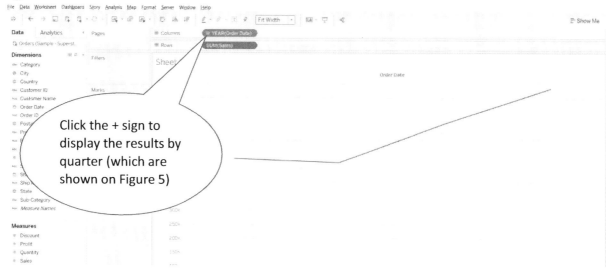

Click the + sign to display the results by quarter (which are shown on Figure 5)

- Expand the + sign, located just before the **Year (Order Date)** in the **Columns** shelf as shown on Figure 4, which will lead to Figure 5

Figure 5

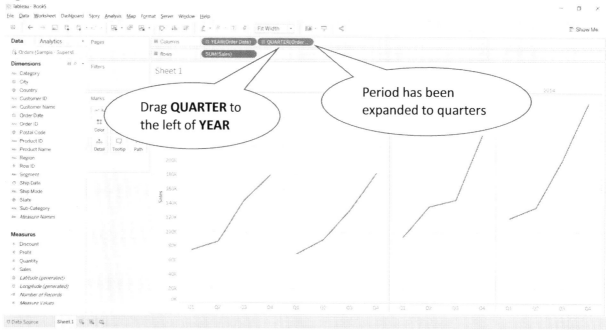

Drag **QUARTER** to the left of **YEAR**

Period has been expanded to quarters

On Figure 5, both quarters and years are in the displayed view. To analyze the performance over various quarters, swap **Quarter** with **Year** by:
- Drag and drop **QUARTER** to the left of **YEAR** on the **Columns** shelf, as shown on Figure 5, which will lead to Figure 6

Figure 6

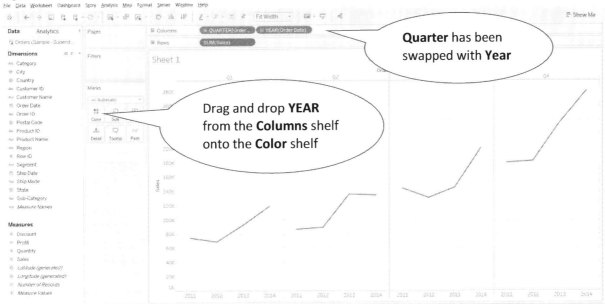

- Drag and drop **YEAR** from the **Columns** shelf onto the **Color** shelf in the **Marks Card**, as shown on Figure 6, which will lead to Figure 7

Figure 7

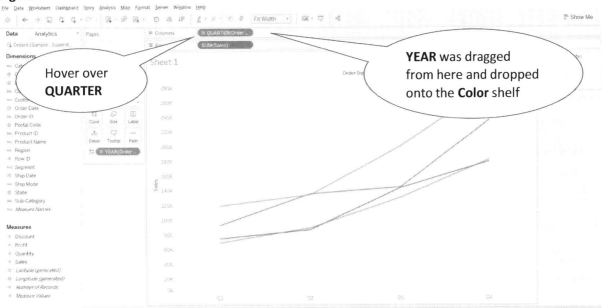

To change the display from **Quarters** to **Months**:
- Hover over **Quarter** in the **Columns** shelf as shown on Figure 7, which will display *Quarter of Order Date* and the pulldown arrow as shown on Figure 8

Figure 8

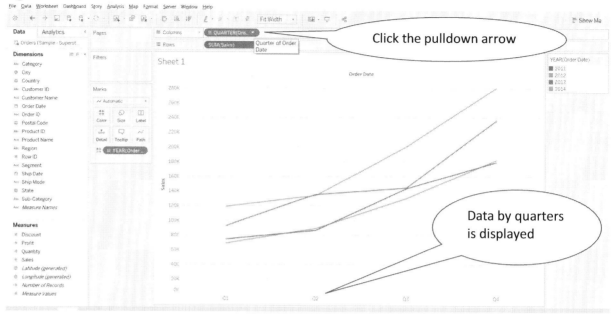

- Click the pulldown arrow displayed on Figure 8, which will lead to the menu tree displayed on Figure 9

Figure 9

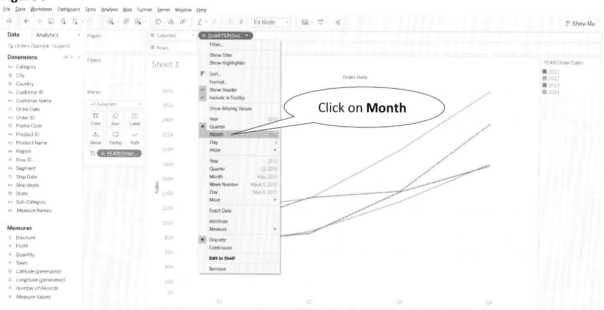

- Click the **Month** menu tree item as shown on Figure 9, which will lead to Figure 10

Figure 10

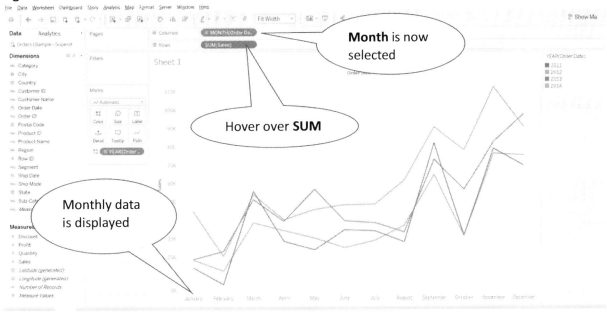

To analyze the **Average** of Sales instead of the **SUM** of Sales (which is shown on Figure 10):

- Hover over **SUM (Sales)** in the **Rows** shelf as shown on Figure 10, which will display a pulldown arrow
- Click the pulldown arrow when it is displayed, which will lead to the menu tree displayed on Figure 11

Figure 11

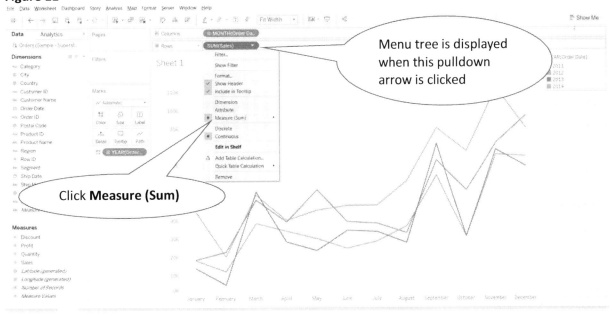

- Click the menu tree item **Measure (Sum)** as shown on Figure 11, which will lead to the secondary menu tree displayed on Figure 12

75

Figure 12

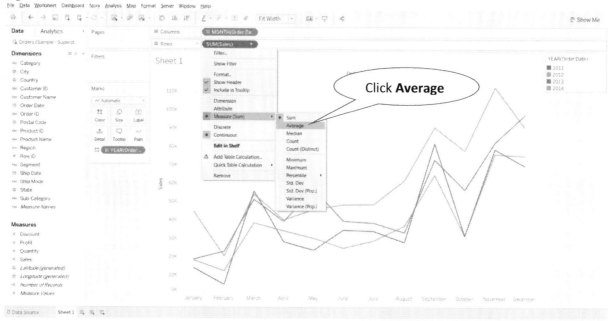

- Click the **Average** menu tree item as shown on Figure 12, which will lead to Figure 13

Figure 13

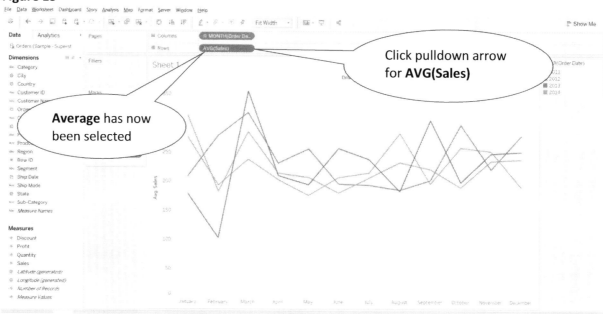

To analyze year-over-year growth:
- Click the pulldown arrow for **AVG(Sales)** in the Rows Shelf as shown on Figure 13
- Click the pulldown arrow when it is displayed, which will lead to Figure 14 where the menu tree is displayed

Figure 14

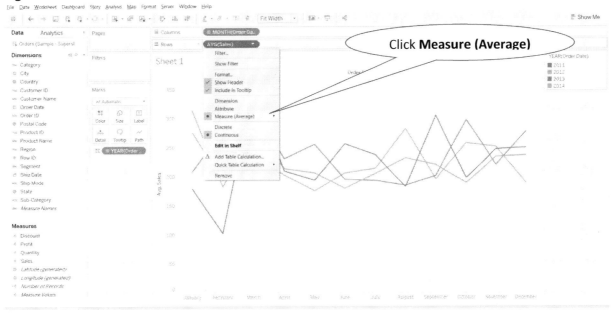

- Click **Measure (Average)** as shown on Figure 14, which will lead to the secondary menu displayed on Figure 15

Figure 15

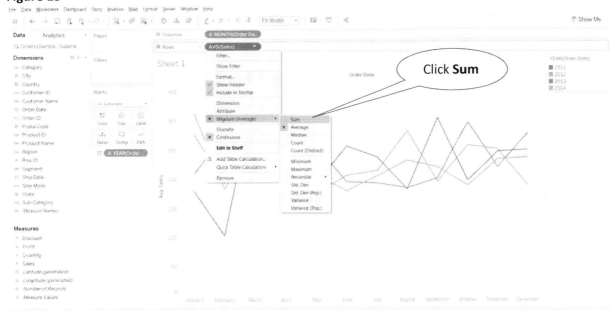

- Click **Sum** as shown on Figure 15, which will lead to the display on Figure 16

Figure 16

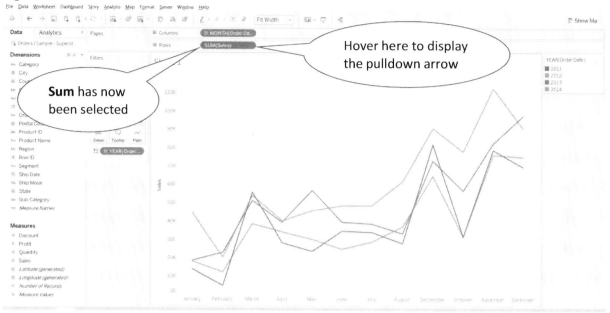

- Hover over **SUM (Sales)** in the **Rows** shelf as shown on Figure 16, which will display a pulldown arrow
- Click the pulldown arrow when it is displayed, which will lead to the menu tree displayed on Figure 17

Figure 17

- Click the **Quick Table Calculation** menu tree item as shown on Figure 17, which will lead to the secondary menu tree displayed on Figure 18

Figure 18

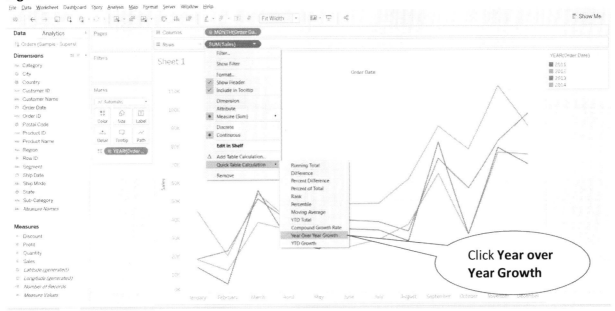

- Click the **Year over Year Growth** menu tree item as shown on Figure 18, which will lead to Figure 19

Figure 19

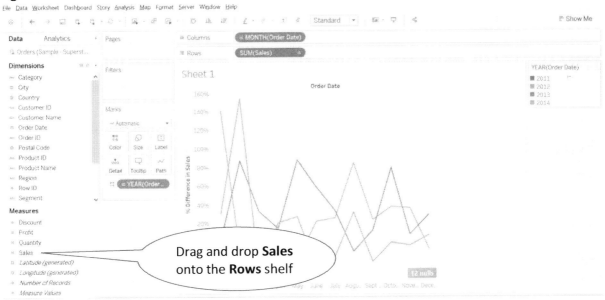

To display the original sales figures on the same chart:
- Drag and drop the **Sales** measure onto the **Rows** shelf as shown on Figure 19, which will lead to Figure 20

Figure 20

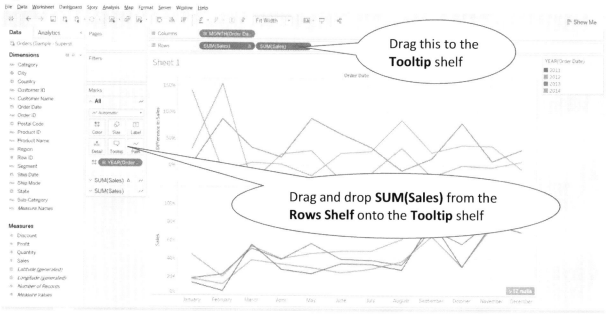

This visualization now enables analysis to be made from two different perspectives (Sales and % Difference in Sales).

To enable values to be displayed when the cursor is placed over an item, i.e., enable hovering:

- Drag **SUM (Sales)** from the **Rows** shelf onto the **Tooltip** shelf (in the **Marks Card** area), as shown on Figure 20, which will lead to Figure 21

Figure 21

- Hover over a line, which will cause its associated data to be displayed as shown on Figure 22

Figure 22

Exercise 11: Crosstab and Swapping

Objective: This exercise will demonstrate how to display visualization data in a crosstab format, as well as swap axes so that data can be viewed from a different perspective

We will start this exercise with Figure 1, which is based on two dimensions (**Category** and **Order Date**) and one measure (**Sales**).

Figure 1

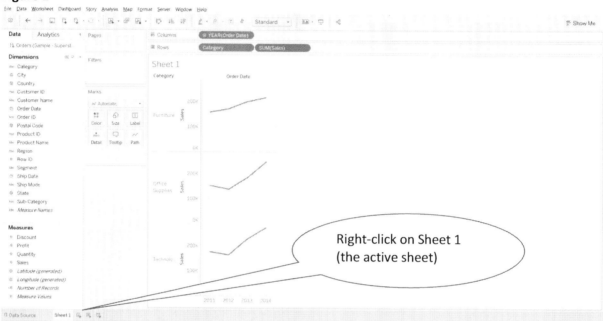

- Right-click the **Sheet 1** tab as shown on Figure 1, which will popup the menu tree displayed on Figure 2

Figure 2

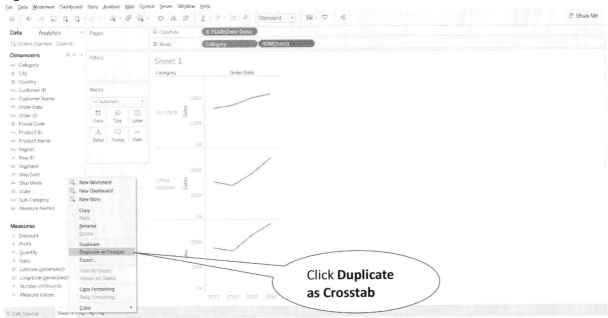

- Click the menu tree item **Duplicate as Crosstab** as shown on Figure 2, which will lead to Figure 3 where the duplicate **Sheet 1(2)** is displayed

Figure 3

- Click on **Sheet 1(2)** as shown on Figure 3, which will lead to Figure 4

Figure 4

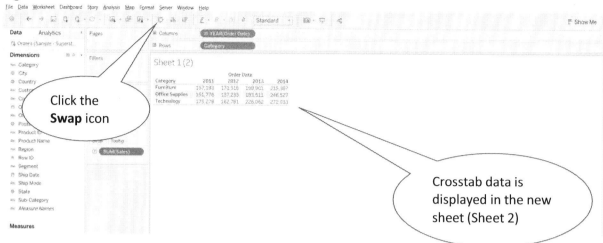

The following steps will demonstrate how to swap axes so that data can be viewed from a different perspective. We will start this exercise with the data displayed on Figure 4.

To perform the axis swap:
- Click the **Swap** icon as shown on Figure 4, which will lead to Figure 5 where the rows have been swapped with the columns

Figure 5

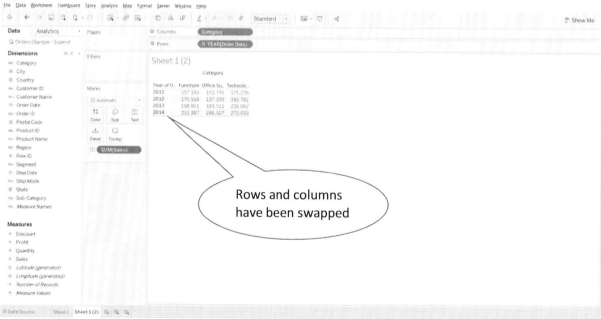

On Figure 5, due to the swap:
- Years are now displayed in the rows
- Categories are now displayed in the columns

Exercise 12: Sorting

Objective: This exercise will demonstrate how to perform the sort function

Note: Use the **Global Superstore** file for this exercise

- Develop the Figure 1 visualization, whose results need to be sorted in descending order

Figure 1

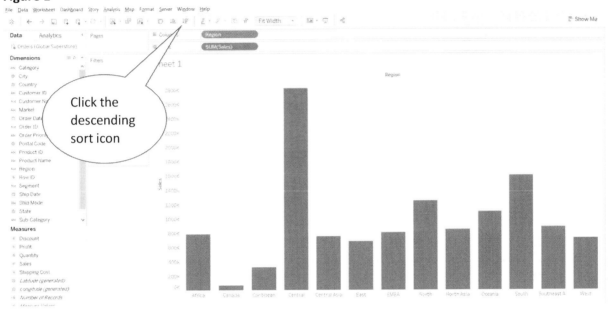

- Click the descending sort icon as shown on Figure 1, which will lead to the display on Figure 2

Figure 2

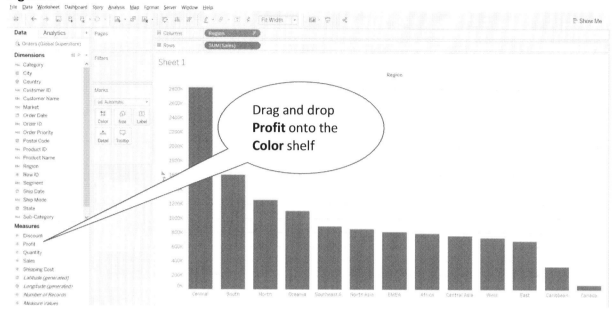

To analyze the results by profitability:
- Drag and drop the **Profit** measure onto the **Color** shelf in the **Marks Card** as shown on Figure 2, which will lead to the display on Figure 3

Figure 3

Color intensity indicates the profitability. For example, while EMEA and Africa sales are nearly equal, Africa is far more profitable (as indicated by the intensity of the blue color). EMEA profit is 43,898, while Africa profit is 88,872. If you want to display the precise profit, just hover over the bar for the desired region.

The next exercise will show how to sort within a sub-category.

Note: Use the **Sample - Superstore** spreadsheet for this exercise

- Develop the Figure 4 visualization

Figure 4

- Click **Sub-category** as shown on Figure 4, which will lead to Figure 5 (where **Sub-Category** is highlighted with a darker shade of blue)

Figure 5

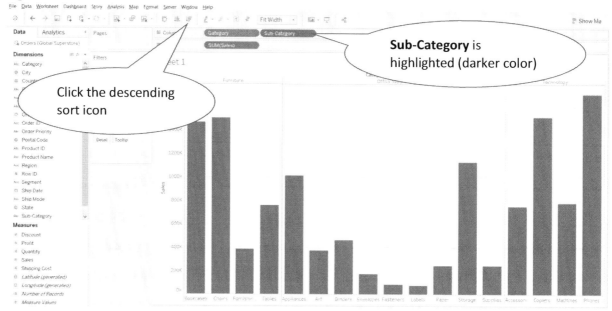

- Click the **Descending sort** icon as shown on Figure 5, which will lead to the display on Figure 6

Figure 6

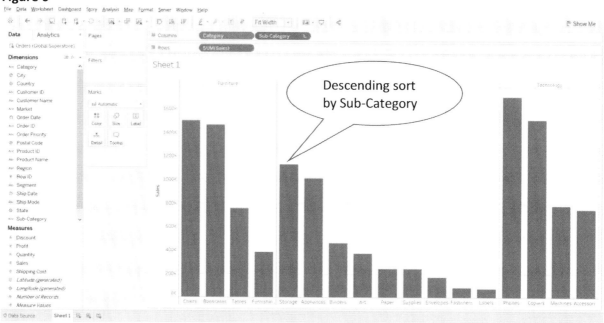

Exercise 13: Sorting (continued)

Objective: This exercise will demonstrate the sort function in more detail

Note: Use the **Global Superstore** file for this exercise

- Develop the Figure 1 visualization, which displays the sum of **Sales** by **Category** and **Sub-Category**.

Figure 1

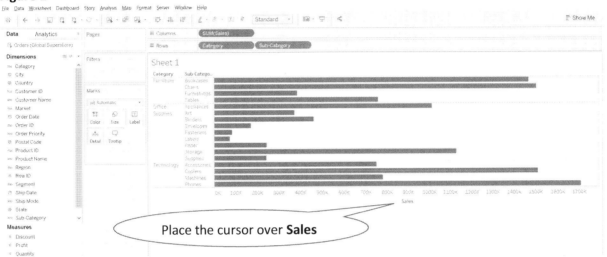

Place the cursor over **Sales**

To sort the displayed data using the **Quick Sort** icon:
- Move the cursor over **Sales** as shown on Figure 1, which will display the **Quick Sort** icon shown on Figure 2

Figure 2

Click the **Quick Sort** icon

- Click the **Quick Sort** icon as shown on Figure 2, which will sort the bars in each category in descending order as displayed on Figure 3

Figure 3

- Click the **Quick Sort** icon again as shown on Figure 3, which will re-sort the bars in ascending order as displayed on Figure 4

Figure 4

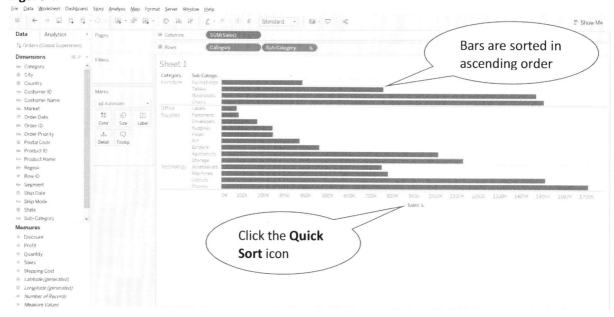

The following steps will demonstrate how to sort using a different method, which enables more options to be selected. We will start with a new visualization, based on the **Global Superstore** spreadsheet, which is displayed on Figure 5.

Figure 5

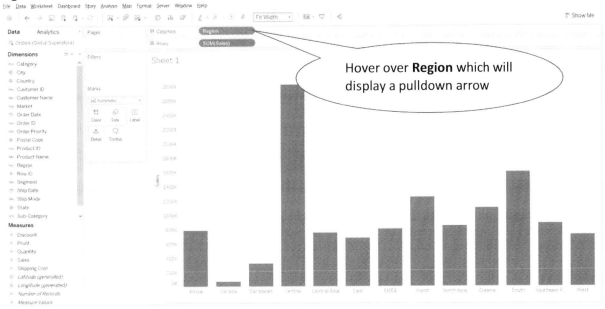

- Hover over **Region** (in the Columns shelf) as shown on Figure 5, which will lead to Figure 6 where the pulldown arrow for the **Region** dimension is displayed

Figure 6

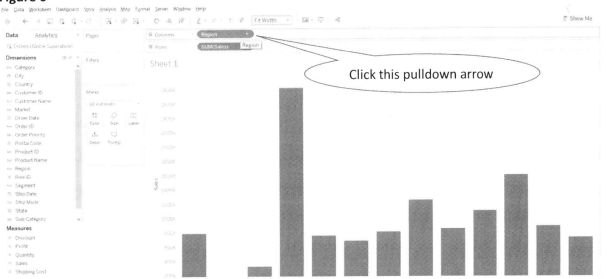

- Click the pulldown arrow when it is displayed, which will lead to the menu tree displayed on Figure 7

Figure 7

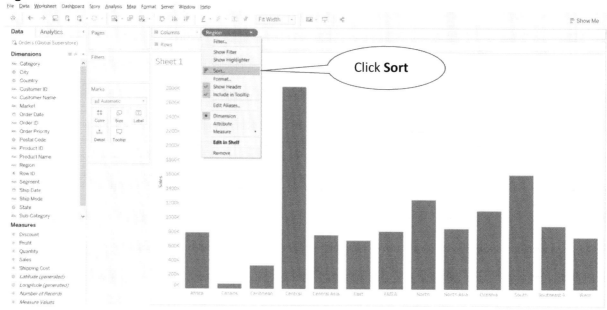

- Click the **Sort** menu tree item as shown on Figure 7, which will popup the box displayed on Figure 8

Figure 8

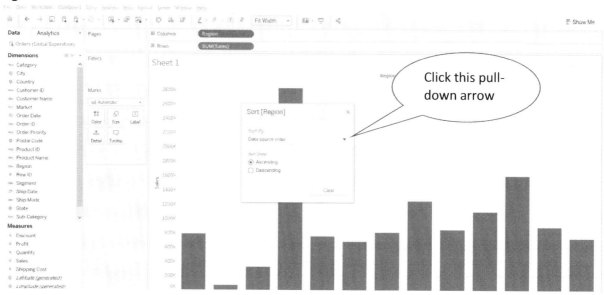

To display the **Sort By** options:

- Click the **Sort By** pulldown arrow as shown on Figure 8, which will display the menu tree shown on Figure 9

Figure 9

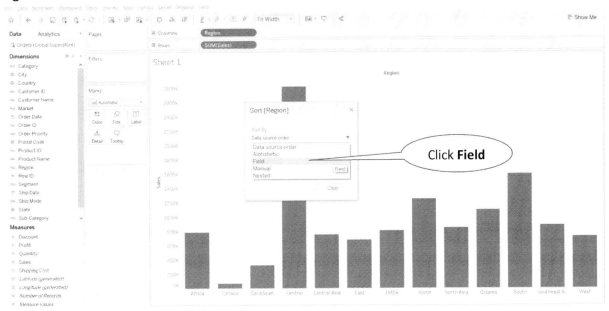

- Click **Field** as shown on Figure 9, which will lead to Figure 10 (where **Field** has been selected)

Figure 10

On Figure 10, **Sales** is the field that is currently selected. To change the field:

- Click the **Field Name** pulldown arrow as shown on Figure 10, which will lead to Figure 11 where the field names are displayed

Figure 11

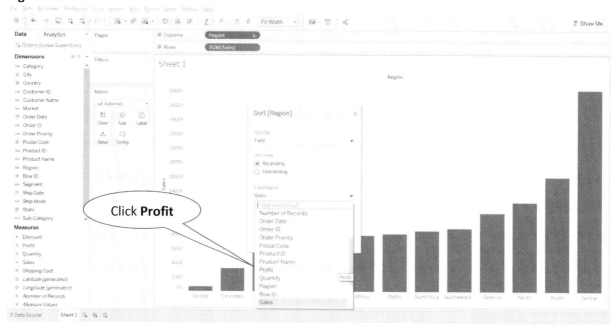

To replace the field **Sales** with **Profit**:

- Click **Profit** as shown on Figure 11, which will lead to Figure 12 where **Profit** is selected

Figure 12

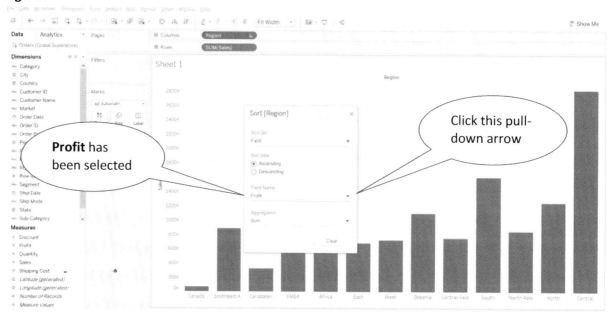

To revert back to the original selection, **Sales**, for the **Field Name**:
- Click the pulldown arrow for **Field Name** as shown on Figure 12
- When the menu tree is displayed, click **Sales** which will lead to Figure 13 where the field name selected is **Sales**

Figure 13

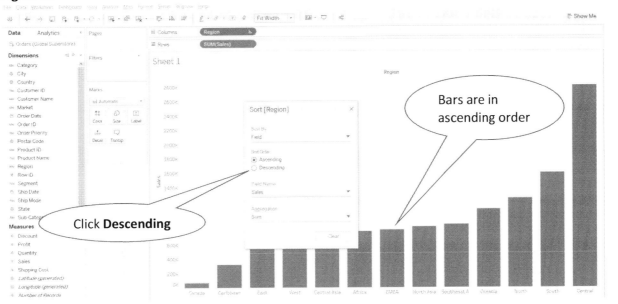

To sort the bars, which are currently in ascending order, in descending order:
- Click **Descending** as shown on Figure 13, which will lead to Figure 14 where the sort order is descending

Figure 14

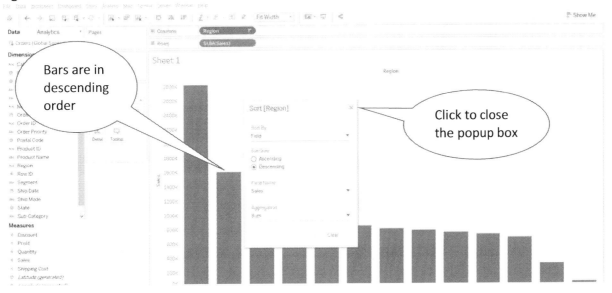

- Click **x** as shown on Figure 14, which will close the **Sort (Region)** popup box

Exercise 14: Drilldown

Objective: This exercise will demonstrate how to display the complete, full data, associated with a displayed visualization

Note: Use the **Global Superstore** file for this exercise

- Develop the Figure 1 visualization, which displays the sum of sales by **Market, Category** and **Sub-Category**

Figure 1

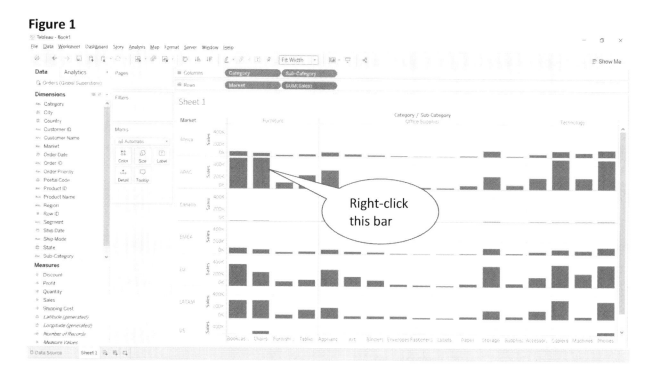

- Right-click the **Furniture** bar for APAC as shown on Figure 1, which will lead to Figure 2 where a menu tree is displayed

Figure 2

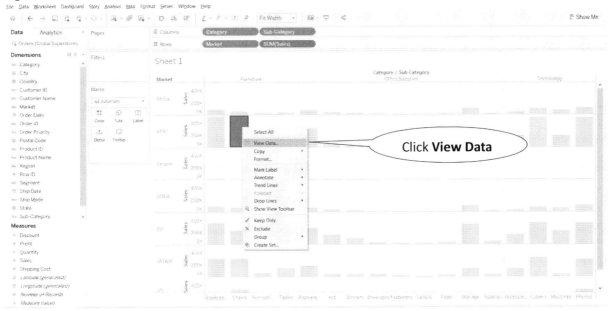

- Click the **View Data** menu tree item as shown on Figure 2, which will popup the **View Data** window shown on Figure 3

Figure 3

- Click the **Full Data** tab as shown on Figure 3, which will lead to Figure 4 where the detailed data is displayed

Figure 4

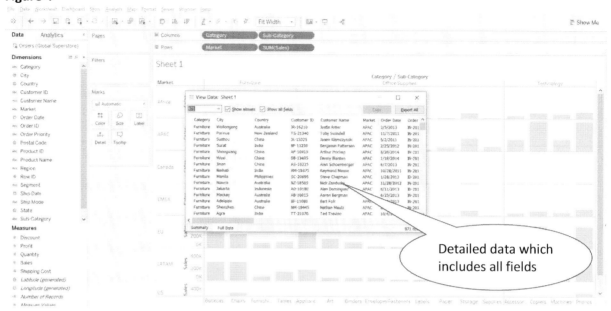

Detailed data which includes all fields

Note that the ability to download data may be limited by the user's authorization.

You can also view the data using another method, which will now be described.

- Develop the visualization shown on Figure 5

Figure 5

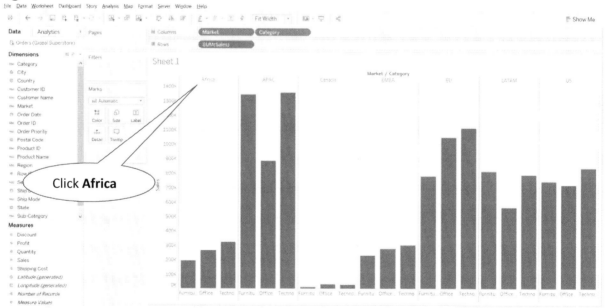

Click **Africa**

To display the data for **Africa**:
- Click **Africa** as shown on Figure 5, which will lead to Figure 6 where a popup box is displayed

Figure 6

- Click the **View Data** icon as shown on Figure 6, which will lead to Figure 7 where the data is displayed

Figure 7

To **Export** the data:
- Click the **Export All** button as shown on Figure 7, which will prompt you to save the data file

If you want to see all the data, rather than just the filtered data, click the **Full Data** tab which is highlighted on Figure 7. After accessing that tab, you will be provided additional options such as **Show Aliases** and **Show all fields**.

Exercise 15: Aggregate Measures

Objective: This exercise will demonstrate how to work with aggregates.

Note: Use the **Global Superstore** file for this exercise

We will start with Figure 1, which displays a blank worksheet.

Figure 1

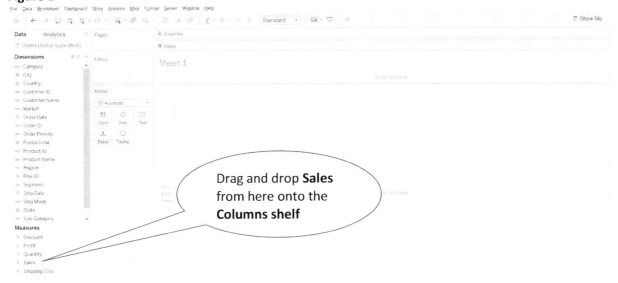

Drag and drop **Sales** from here onto the **Columns shelf**

- Drag and drop **Sales** onto the **Columns shelf** as shown on Figure 1, which will lead to Figure 2

Figure 2

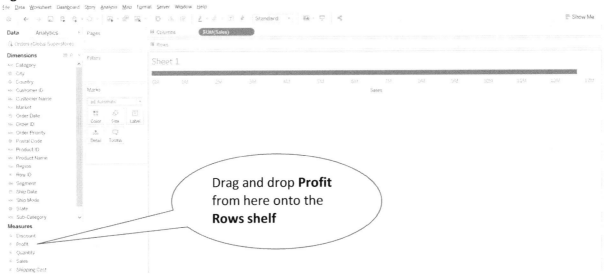

Drag and drop **Profit** from here onto the **Rows shelf**

- Drag and drop **Profit** onto the **Rows shelf** as shown on Figure 2, which will lead to Figure 3 where the aggregated value is highlighted

Figure 3

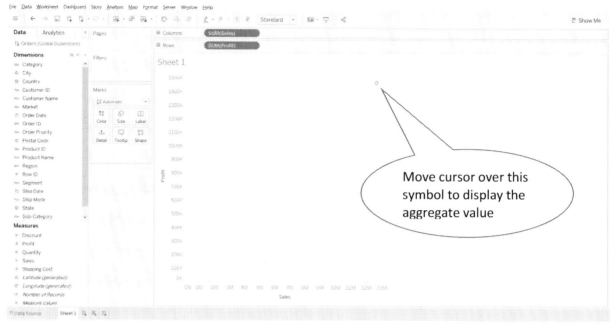

To display the aggregate value:
- Move cursor over the aggregate symbol as shown on Figure 3, which will lead to Figure 4 where the exact value for the total sales and total profit is displayed

Figure 4

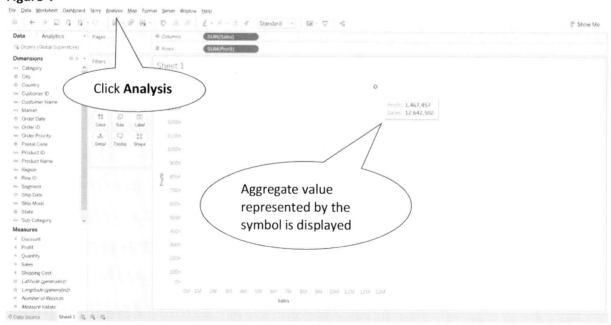

To deaggregate and display individual values:

- Click **Analysis** on the **Menu Bar** as shown on Figure 4, which will popup the menu tree displayed on Figure 5

Figure 5

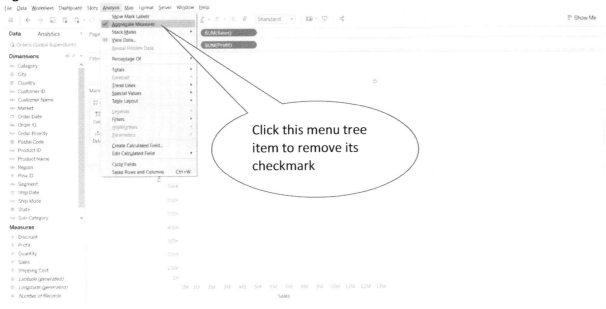

To remove the checkmark for **Aggregate Measures**:

- Click the **Aggregate Measures** menu tree item as shown on Figure 5, which will lead to Figure 6

Figure 6

To display the value for any symbol on the chart:

- Hover over the symbol as shown on Figure 6, which will lead to Figure 7

Figure 7

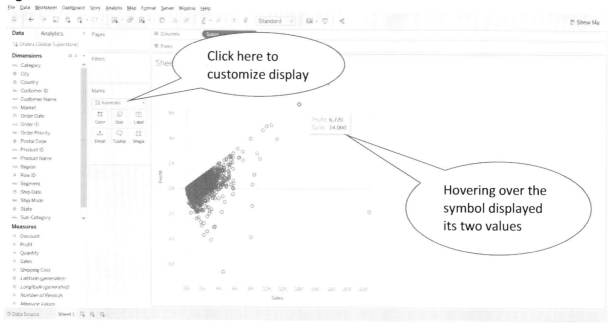

- Click on **Automatic** in the **Marks Card** as shown on Figure 7, which will display the menu tree shown on Figure 8

Figure 8

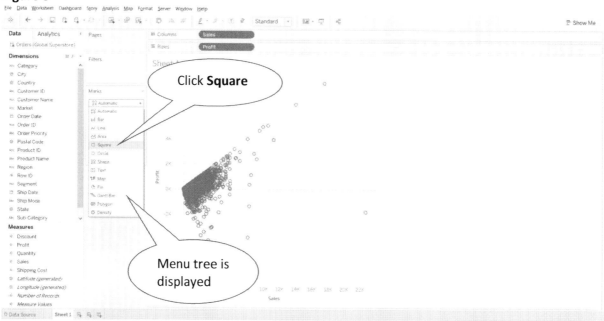

- Click the **Square** menu tree item as shown on Figure 8, which will lead to Figure 9

Figure 9

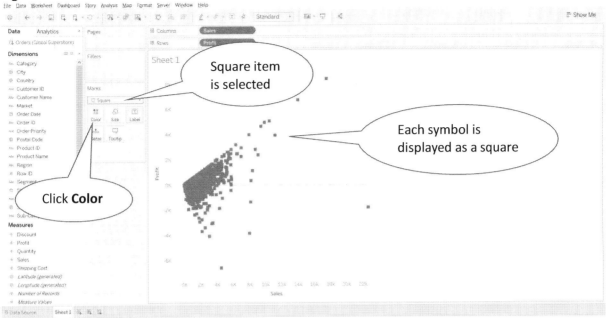

- Click **Color** on the **Marks Card** as shown on Figure 9, which will lead to Figure 10

Figure 10

- Click the green color as shown on Figure 10, which will lead to Figure 11 where the color has changed to green (from blue)

Figure 11

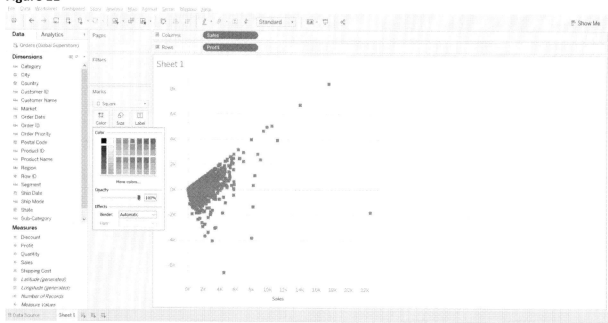

Chapter 4: Filtering

Exercise 16: Exclude and Keep Only

Objective: This exercise will demonstrate the use of the Exclude and Keep Only functions

Note: Use the **Sample - Superstore** spreadsheet for this exercise

- Develop the Figure 1 visualization, which shows a chart with the sum of sales for four regions

Figure 1

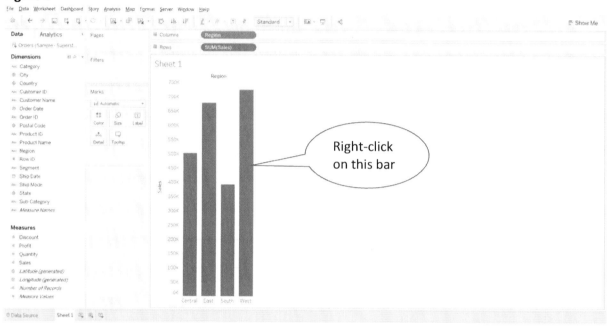

Suppose we want to exclude the sales for a specific region and only focus on the sales for the remaining three regions. In other words, we want to "exclude" one region from the analysis. The following steps will show how this can be done.

To exclude the **West** region:
- Right-click on the 4th bar (i.e. for the West region, which needs to be excluded), as shown on Figure 1, which will popup the menu tree displayed on Figure 2

Figure 2

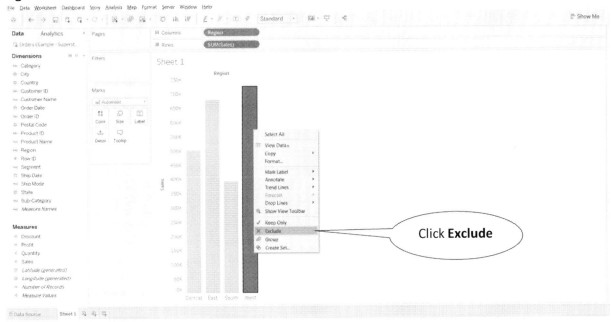

- Click **Exclude** as shown on Figure 2, which will lead to Figure 3, where the results are limited to the remaining three regions

Figure 3

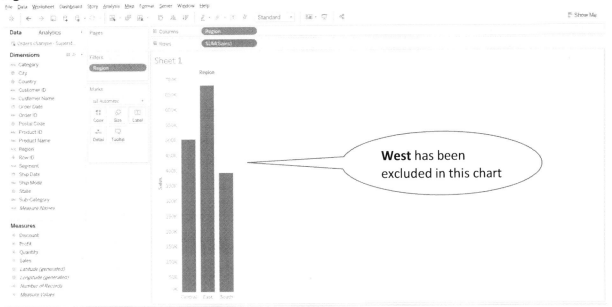

West has been excluded in this chart

Another useful Tableau function is **"Keep."** It can be used to retain selected items while excluding all the other displayed items, as shown in the next procedure.

We will start with Figure 4, which displays the sum of sales for various sub-categories.

Figure 4

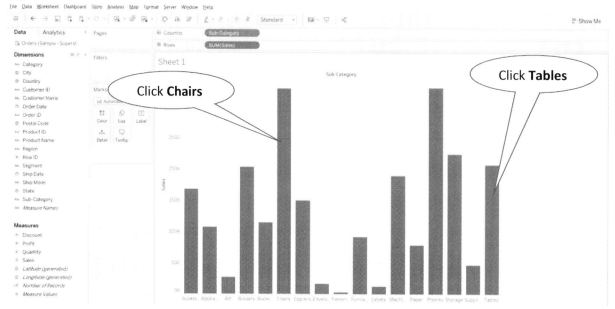

If you want to analyze the sales for only two items, Tables and Chairs, hold down the **Ctrl** key and then:
- Click the Tables bar (on a Mac, use Apple + Click)
- Click the Chairs bar (on a Mac, use Apple + Click)

This will lead to Figure 5, where two bars are selected and highlighted. Notice the small popup window, which displays the **Keep Only** and **Exclude** options.

Figure 5

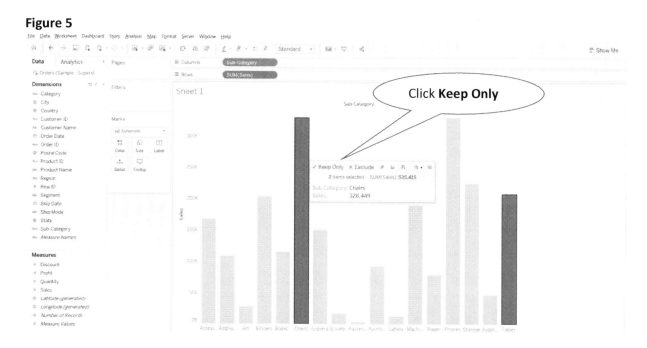

- Click **Keep Only** on the popup box as shown on Figure 5, which will lead to Figure 6

Figure 6

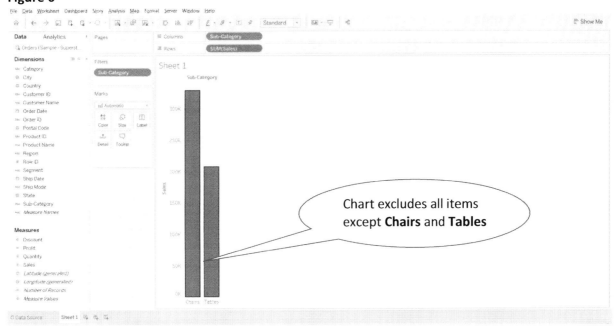

Chart excludes all items except **Chairs** and **Tables**

Exercise 17: Filtering on the Filter Shelf

Objective: This exercise will demonstrate how to filter using the Filter Shelf

Note: Use the **Global Superstore** file for this exercise

- Develop the Figure 1 visualization, which displays the sum of sales for various regions

Figure 1

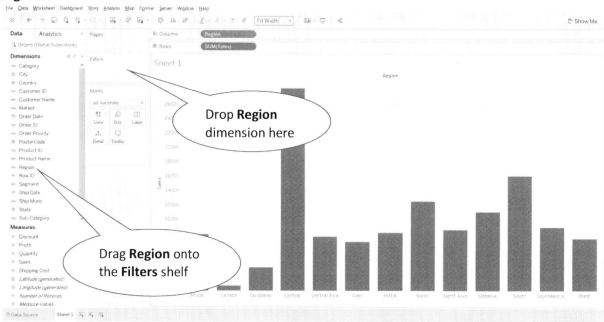

- Drag and drop **Region** from the **Data Window** onto the **Filters** shelf as shown on Figure 1, which will popup the **Filter (Region)** window displayed on Figure 2

Note: On a Mac, the procedure to drag and drop may vary slightly.

Figure 2

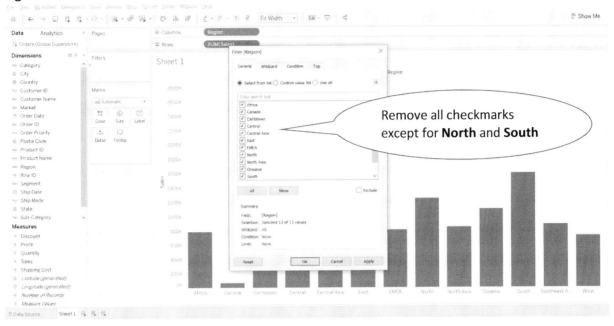

- Remove all checkmarks with the exception of **North** and **South** as shown on Figure 2, which will lead to Figure 3

Figure 3

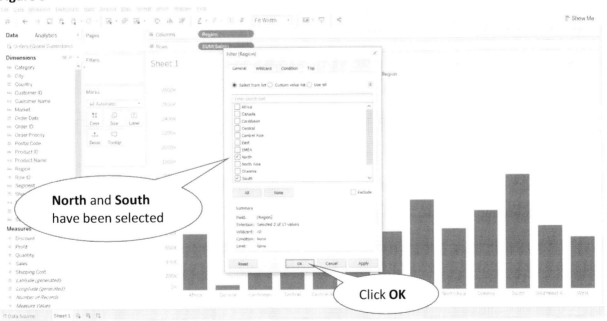

- Click **OK** as shown on Figure 3, which will lead to Figure 4 where the filtered data is displayed

Figure 4

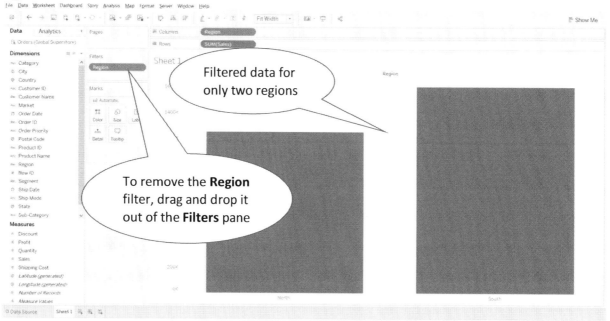

To remove a filter:
* Drag and drop the filter out of the **Filters** shelf as shown on Figure 4, which will lead to Figure 5

Figure 5

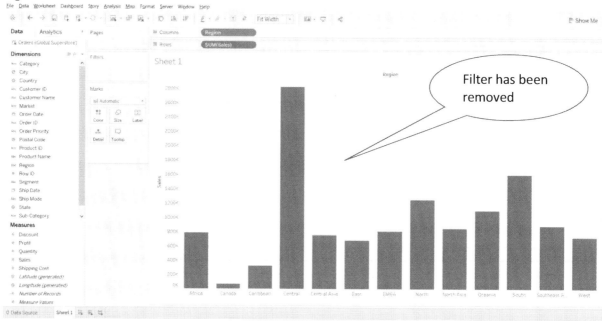

Another method can also be used to remove a filter. In this case, we will start with Figure 6, which shows the North and South region filter in place. Note that Figure 6 is the same as Figure 4.

Figure 6

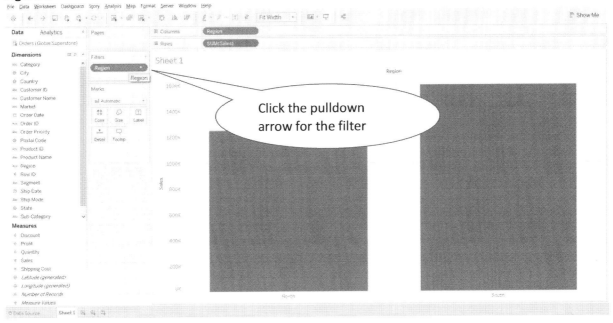

- Click the pulldown arrow for the **Region** filter as shown on Figure 6, which will popup the menu tree displayed on Figure 7

Figure 7

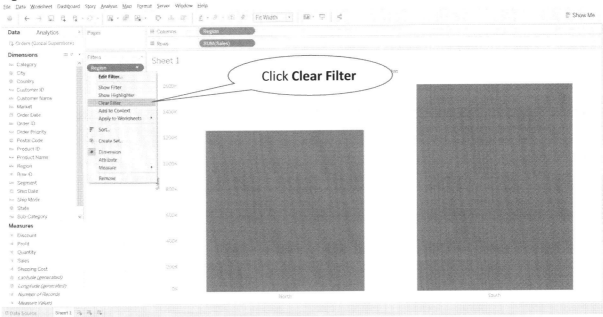

- Click the menu tree item **Clear Filter,** which will remove the filter and lead to Figure 8 where the filter has been removed

Figure 8

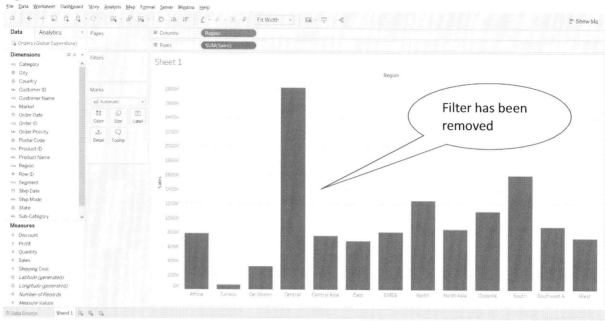

Exercise 18: Quick Filters

Objective: This exercise will demonstrate how a Quick Filter can be created and used.

Note: Use the **Sample - Superstore** spreadsheet for this exercise

- Develop the Figure 1 visualization, which displays a view based on Category, Region and Sales.

Figure 1

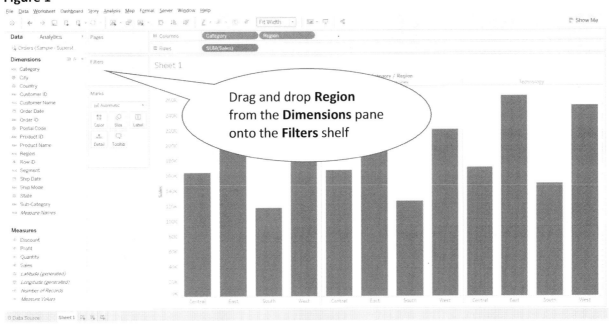

Quick filters enable users to focus on smaller datasets so that they can perform analysis from different perspectives.

To add a quick filter:
- Click **Region** in the **Dimensions** pane
- Drag and drop **Region** onto the **Filters** shelf as shown on Figure 1, which will popup the **Filter (Region)** window displayed on Figure 2

Figure 2

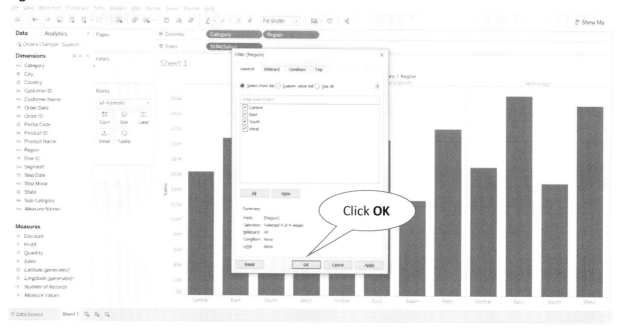

If the default values displayed on the popup window are to be accepted as-is:

- Click **OK** as shown on Figure 2, which will lead to Figure 3

Note: Since all 4 regions were selected on Figure 2, Figure 3 data does not have any filtered data. As an example, if you want to display data only for **Central** and **South**, remove the checkmarks for **East** and **West**. In this step, we will retain all the checkmarks.

Figure 3

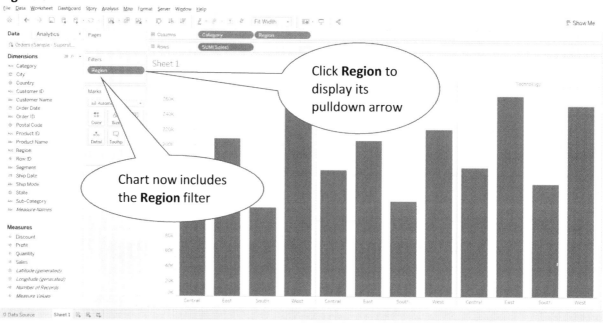

The Quick Filter is not displayed on Figure 3. To display it so that it is available for easy access:
- Click **Region** in the **Filters** shelf as shown on Figure 3, which will display its pulldown arrow
- Click the pulldown arrow when it is displayed, which will lead to the menu tree displayed on Figure 4

Figure 4

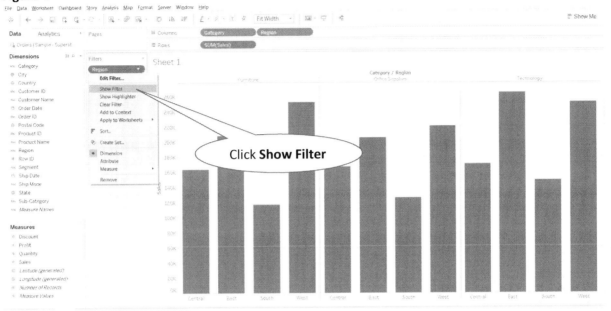

- Click **Show Filter** as shown on Figure 4, which will lead to Figure 5 where the Region **Quick Filter** is displayed

Figure 5

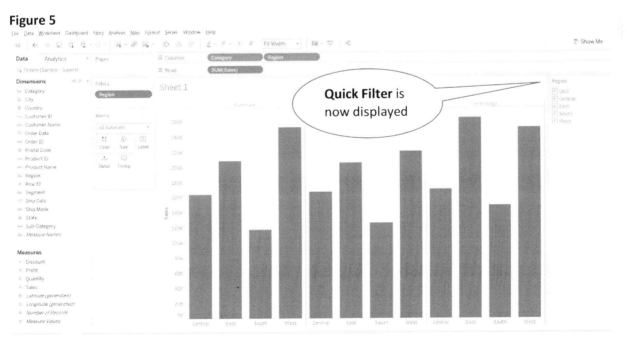

Items in the **Quick Filter** can be selected or deselected by adding or removing a checkmark next to the desired item. For example, the checkmarks next to **Central** and **West** can be deselected, which will limit the analysis to the remaining two regions (**East** and **South**).

Figure 6 shows that two items have been deselected from the **Region** quick filter: Central and West. Hence, the displayed results are limited to the remaining two regions: East and South.

Figure 6

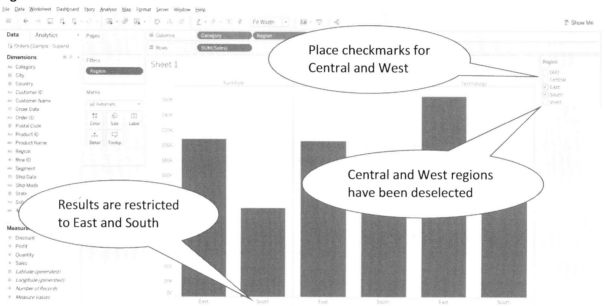

- Place checkmarks for Central and West as shown on Figure 6, which will lead to Figure 7 where all 4 regions are selected

Figure 7

A **Quick Filter** can be added for any dimension contained in the **Data Window**. To add a Quick Filter for **Category** in the visualization displayed on Figure 7:

- Hover over **Category** in the **Data Window** as shown on Figure 7, which will display its pulldown arrow

When the pulldown arrow is displayed:

- Click the pulldown arrow, which will display its menu tree (**Add to Sheet**) shown on Figure 8

Figure 8

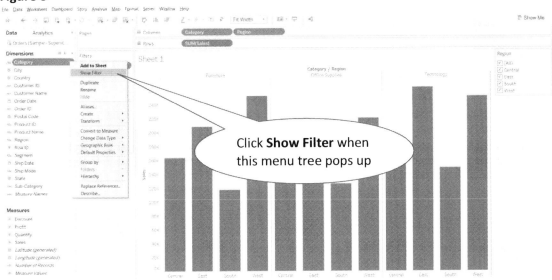

- Click **Show Filter** as shown on Figure 8, which will lead to Figure 9 where the **Category** Quick Filter has been added

Figure 9

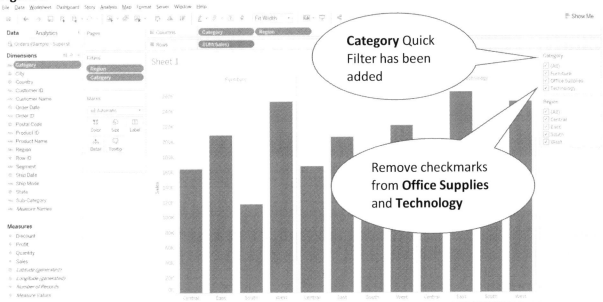

If you want to display the results only for the **Furniture** category (i.e., filter out the data for **Office Supplies** and **Technology)**:

- Deselect **Office Supplies** and **Technology,** by removing their associated checkmarks from the **Category** Quick Filter as shown on Figure 9, which will lead to Figure 10

Figure 10

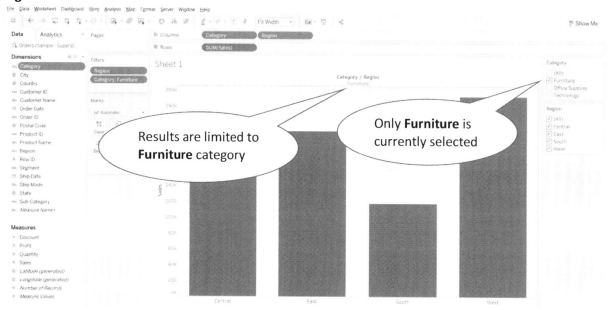

Quick Filters can be removed when they are not needed. Figure 11 shows two Quick Filters in place: **Category** and **Region**.

Figure 11

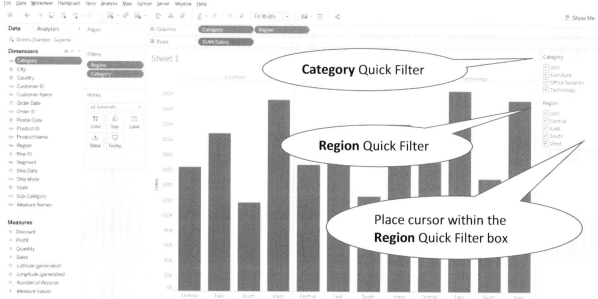

To remove the **Region** Quick filter from Figure 11:

- Place cursor within the **Region** Quick Filter box as shown on Figure 11, which will display the pulldown arrow shown on Figure 12

Figure 12

- Click the pulldown arrow as shown on Figure 12, which will popup the menu tree displayed on Figure 13

Figure 13

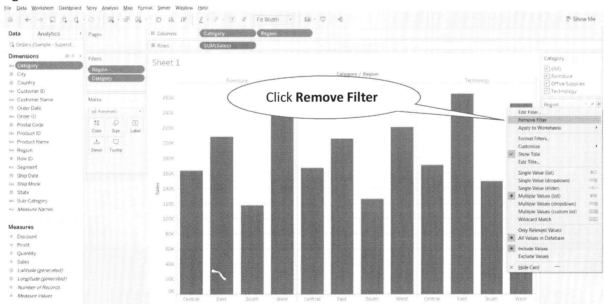

- Click **Remove Filter** as shown on Figure 13, which will lead to Figure 14 where the filter has been removed

Figure 14

Exercise 19: Customizing Quick Filters

Objective: This exercise will demonstrate the Customize and Edit Title Quick Filter features

Note: Use the **Global Superstore** file for this exercise

- Develop the Figure 1 visualization, which is based on market, order priority, category, sub-category and sum of sales

Figure 1

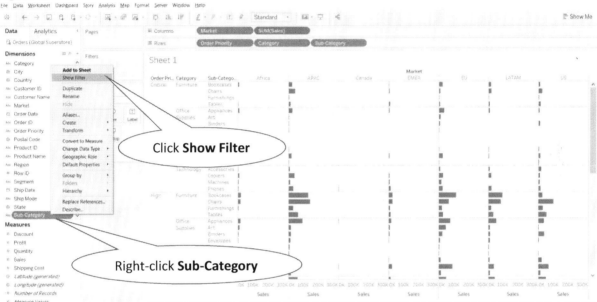

After developing the Figure 1 visualization:
- Right-click **Sub-Category** as shown on Figure 1, which will popup the menu tree displayed on Figure 1

When the menu tree pops-up:
- Click the **Show Filter** menu tree item, which will lead to Figure 2

Figure 2

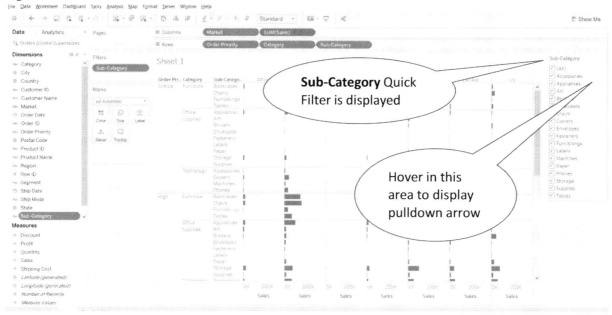

To display the pulldown arrow for the **Sub-Category** Quick Filter:

- Hover within the **Sub-Category** Quick Filter area as shown on Figure 2, which will display the pulldown arrow shown on Figure 3

Figure 3

- Click the pulldown arrow for the **Quick Filter** as shown on Figure 3, which will popup the menu tree displayed on Figure 4

Figure 4

- Click the **Apply to Worksheets** menu tree item as shown on Figure 4, which will lead to the secondary menu tree shown on Figure 5

Figure 5

The menu highlighted on Figure 5 displays three options for applying the Quick Filter. By selecting the appropriate sub-menu tree item, the Quick Filter can be applied to the selected worksheet or the currently displayed worksheet. On Figure 5, the **Only this Worksheet** menu tree item, which is the default, has been selected. Therefore, the Quick Filter will only apply to the currently displayed worksheet (and not to any other worksheets in the current workbook).

We will now navigate through some commonly used items displayed on the Quick Filter menu tree.

Figure 6

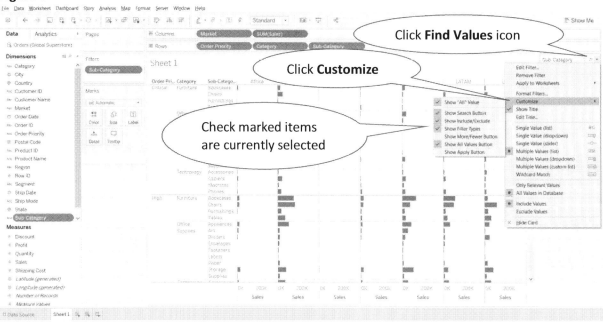

Figure 6 displays various options for the **Customize** menu item:
- Click **Customize** which will popup the sub-menu tree shown on Figure 6, where 5 out of the 7 displayed items are currently checkmarked and, hence, selected

Each of these sub-menu tree items enable useful functions. For example, if a list is very long, the search box can be used to narrow the search.

To access the search box:
- Click the **Find Values** icon as shown on Figure 6, which will open a small box, displayed on Figure 7, where the name to be searched can be typed in

Figure 7

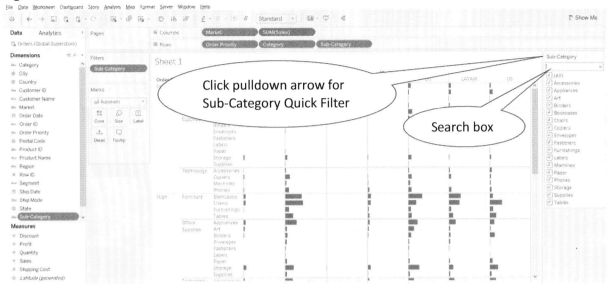

- Click the pulldown arrow for the **Quick Filter** as shown on Figure 7

When the pulldown arrow is displayed:
- Navigate to the **Customize** menu tree which is displayed on Figure 8

On Figure 8, the 7th item on the **Customize** sub-menu tree, **Show Apply Button**, is unchecked. This item is used to display or hide the **Apply** button.

Figure 8

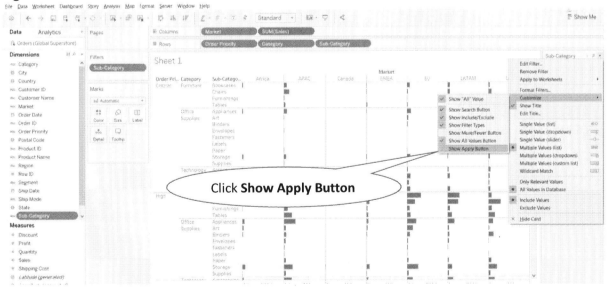

To display the **Apply** button:
- Click **Show Apply Button** as shown on Figure 8, which will lead to Figure 9

Figure 9

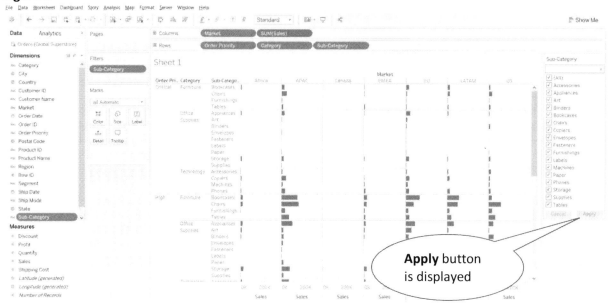

The Apply button is currently greyed out. However, when a selection is made, such as removing a checkmark, the button will be highlighted and become active.

A Quick Filter title can be edited to make it more meaningful or to provide a prompt to the users. We will start with Figure 10.

Figure 10

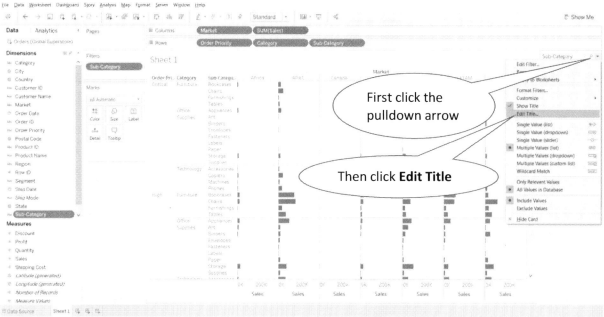

To edit the Quick Filter title:

- Click the Quick Filter's pulldown arrow as shown on Figure 10, which will popup the menu tree displayed on Figure 10
- Click **Edit Title** as shown on Figure 10, which will popup the **Edit Filter Title** box displayed on Figure 11

Figure 11

- Rename the default title to **Select a Sub-Category** as shown on Figure 11, by typing in the new title, which will lead to Figure 12

Figure 12

- Click **OK** after the title has been renamed as shown on Figure 12, which will lead to Figure 13

Figure 13

Renaming the filter title will provide the prompt, **Select a Sub-Category**, to the users as shown on Figure 13, which will make the visualization more user-friendly.

Exercise 20: Quick Filter Single and Multiple Value Lists

Objective: This exercise will demonstrate how single and multiple value lists can be used in quick filters

Note: Use the **Global Superstore** file for this exercise

Tableau provides many options, single or multiple, for displaying the values in a Quick Filter. These will be introduced in this exercise.

- Develop the visualization shown on Figure 1

Figure 1

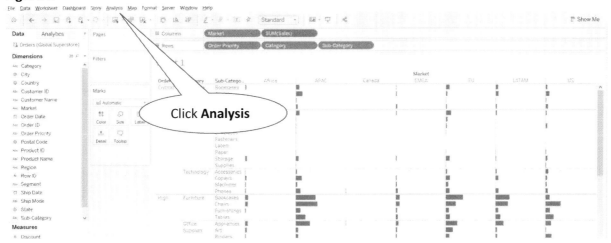

- Click **Analysis** as shown on Figure 1, which will lead to Figure 2

Figure 2

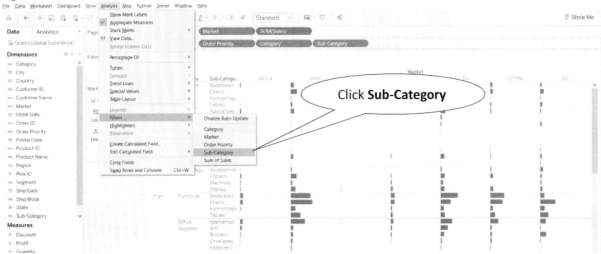

- Navigate as shown on Figure 2 (***Analysis > Filters > Sub-Category***), which will lead to Figure 3 where the **Sub-Category** filter is displayed

Figure 3

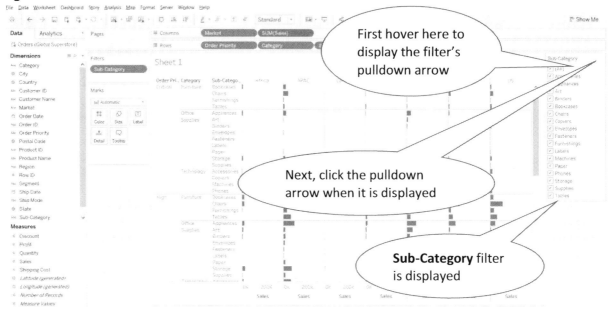

The type of filter displayed on Figure 3 is called the **Multiple Values (list)**. Using checkmarks, individual items can selected or deselected.

The type of filter displayed can be changed easily as demonstrated in the following procedure.

On Figure 3:
- Hover in the **Sub-Category** filter area, which will display its pulldown arrow (shown on Figure 4)
- Click the pulldown arrow when it is displayed, which will lead to Figure 5 where the menu tree is displayed

Figure 4

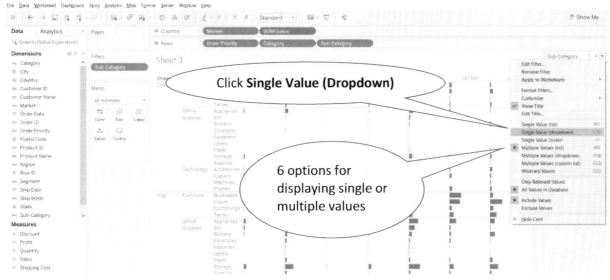

To display the Single Value (dropdown) Quick Filter:
- Click the **Single Value (dropdown)** menu tree item as shown on Figure 4, which will lead to Figure 5

Figure 5

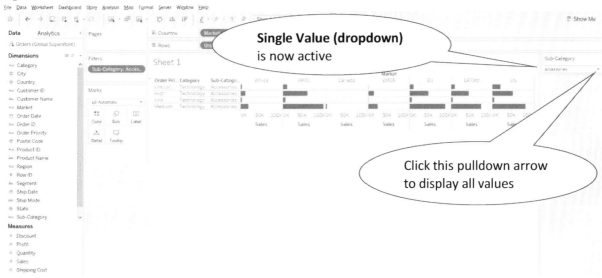

To display all the available values:
- Click the pulldown arrow next to **Accessories** as shown on Figure 5, which will lead to Figure 6

Figure 6

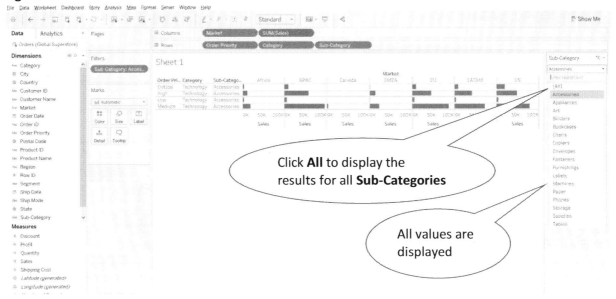

- Click **All** as shown on Figure 6, which will lead to Figure 7 where the results are displayed for all Sub-Categories

Figure 7

Another menu tree option is the **Single Value (List)**, which can be displayed using the following steps:
- Hover in the filter area as shown on Figure 7
- Click the pulldown arrow when it is displayed, which will lead to Figure 8

Figure 8

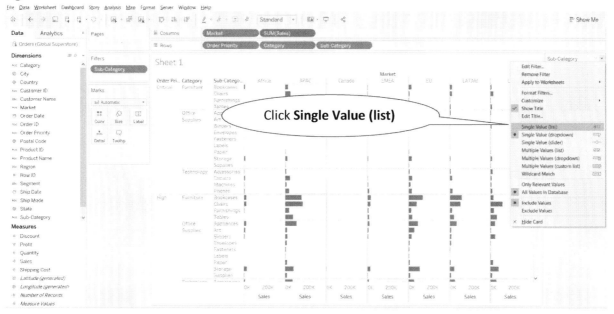

- Click **Single Value (list)** as shown on Figure 8, which will lead to Figure 9

Figure 9

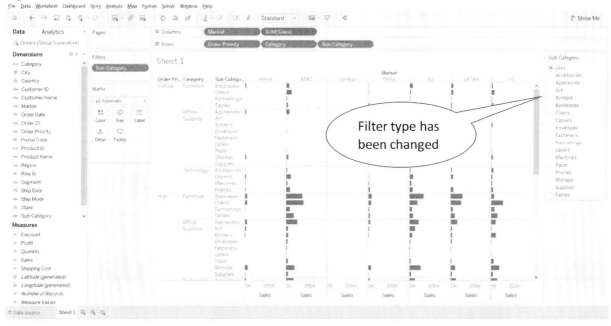

In this case, only a single value can be selected, as the system will only allow one radio button to be checked at any time. If multiple selections need to be made, then the **Multiple Values (List)** option can be used (as shown on Figure 3).

Exercise 21: Slider Quick Filter

Objective: This exercise will demonstrate how sliders can be setup and used

Note: Use the **Global Superstore** file for this exercise

A slider is used when a range needs to be specified dynamically.

- Develop the visualization shown on Figure 1, where the **Sub-Category** Quick Filter is displayed.

Figure 1

- Click the **Quick Filter** pulldown arrow as shown on Figure 1, which will popup the menu tree displayed on Figure 2

Figure 2

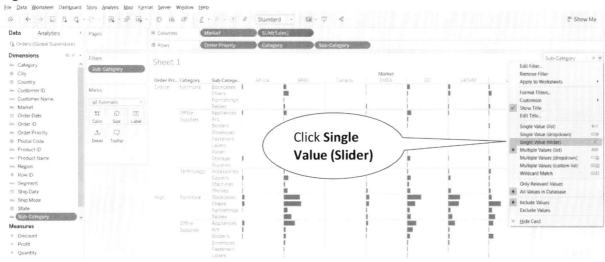

To setup a single value slider:
- Click the **Single Value (Slider)** menu tree item as shown on Figure 2, which will lead to Figure 3

Figure 3

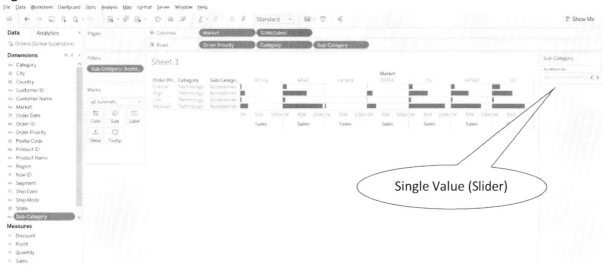

The slider in Figure 3 can be moved to the left or right, as needed, to dynamically change the range being analyzed.

A multiple value slider contains two sliders, which can be used to dynamically specify the low and high range values. The following procedure will show you how to setup a multiple value slider.

- Develop the visualization shown on Figure 4

Figure 4

Expand the period to days:

- Click the + sign for **Year(Order Date)** in **Columns** as shown on Figure 4
- Click the + signs for **Quarter** and **Month** (when they are displayed)**,** which will lead to Figure 5

Figure 5

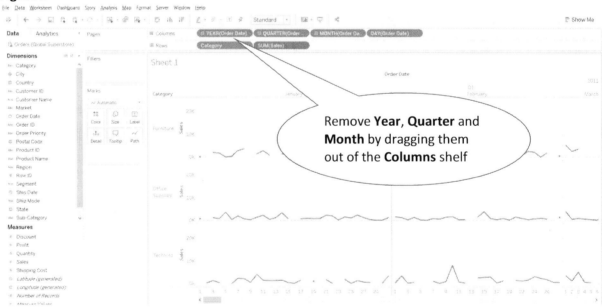

- Remove **Year**, **Quarter** and **Month** by dragging them out of the **Columns** shelf, as shown on Figure 5, which will lead to Figure 6

Figure 6

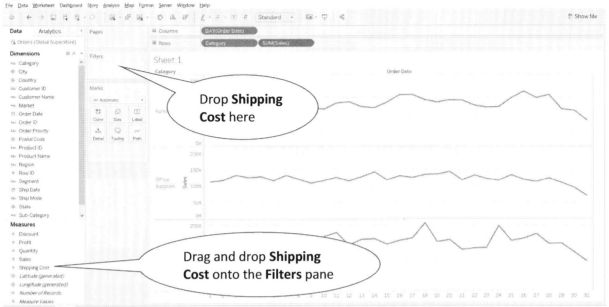

To setup a multiple value slider:
- Drag and drop the **Shipping Cost** measure onto the **Filters** pane as shown on Figure 6, which will cause the **Filter Field (Shipping Cost)** window to popup as displayed on Figure 7

Figure 7

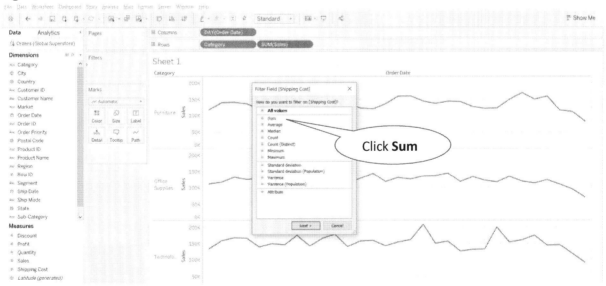

- Click **Sum** as shown on Figure 7, which will lead to Figure 8 where the **Sum** measure is selected and highlighted

Figure 8

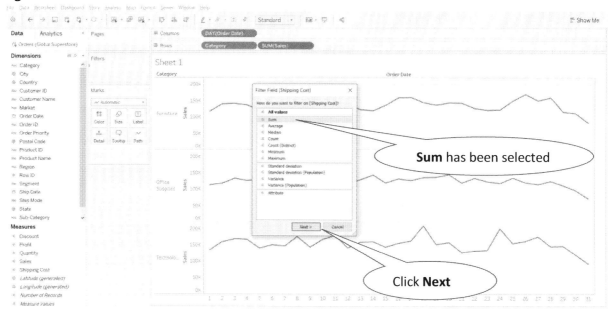

- Click **Next** as shown on Figure 8, which will popup the **Filter (Shipping Cost)** window displayed on Figure 9

Figure 9

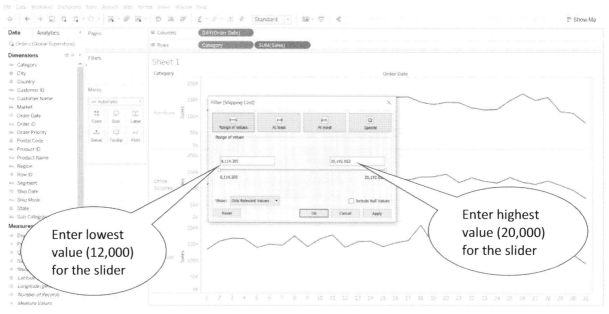

- Enter the lowest value, 12,000, for the slider range in the field highlighted on Figure 9
- Enter the highest value, 20,000, for the slider range in the field highlighted on Figure 9

Figure 10 shows that the lowest and the highest values have been entered.

Figure 10

- Click **OK** as shown on Figure 10, which will lead to the display on Figure 11

Figure 11

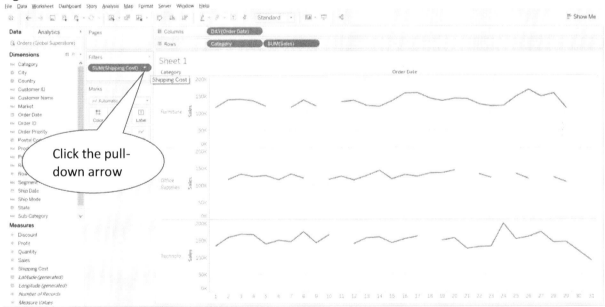

The Quick Filter slider is not currently displayed though it is active. To display the filter:
- Hover over the **SUM (Shipping Cost)** filter, which will display its pulldown arrow (shown on Figure 11)

143

When the pulldown arrow for **SUM (Shipping Cost)** is displayed in the **Filter** pane:
- Click the pulldown arrow as shown on Figure 11, which will popup the menu tree displayed on Figure 12

Figure 12

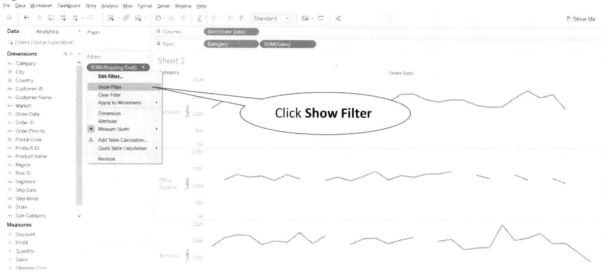

- Click **Show Filter** as shown on Figure 12, which will lead to Figure 13 where the slider is displayed

Figure 13

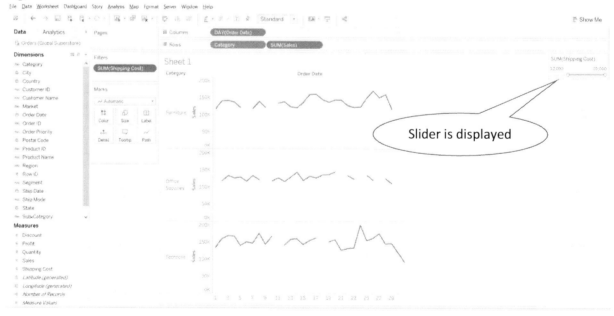

Chapter 5: Exporting

Exercise 22: Export to PDF

Objective: This exercise will demonstrate how to save a visualization in PDF format

- Develop the visualization shown on Figure 1, which we will save in the PDF format

Figure 1

- Click **File** on the **Menu Bar** as shown on Figure 1, which will lead to the menu tree displayed on Figure 2

Figure 2

- Click the **Print to PDF** menu tree item as shown on Figure 2, which will popup the **Print to PDF** window displayed on Figure 3

Figure 3

Click **OK** after selecting the desired options

- Click the **Landscape** radio button, if needed

After the desired selections have been made on the **Print to PDF** popup window on Figure 3:
- Click **OK** as shown on Figure 3, which will popup the **Save PDF** window displayed on Figure 4

Figure 4

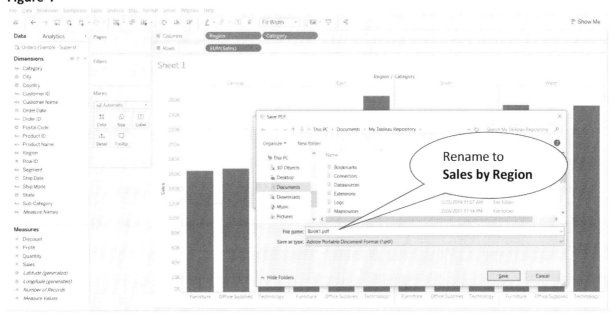

Rename to **Sales by Region**

- Rename the default file name, **Book 1**, to **Sales by Region** as shown on Figure 4, which will lead to Figure 5

Figure 5

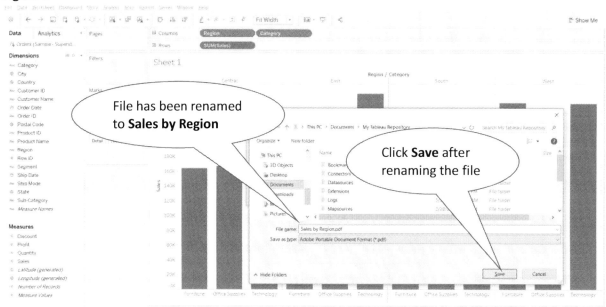

- Click **Save** as shown on Figure 5, which will lead to Figure 6 (which contains the PDF display in a separate window)

Figure 6

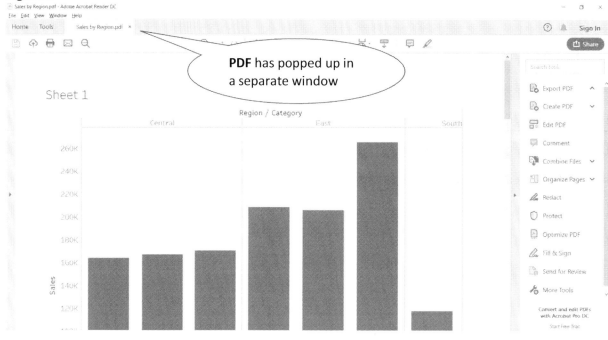

Exercise 23: Export to PowerPoint

Objective: This exercise will demonstrate how to copy and export a displayed image

Note: Use the **Global Superstore** file for this exercise

- Develop the visualization shown on Figure 1, which we will export as an image

Figure 1

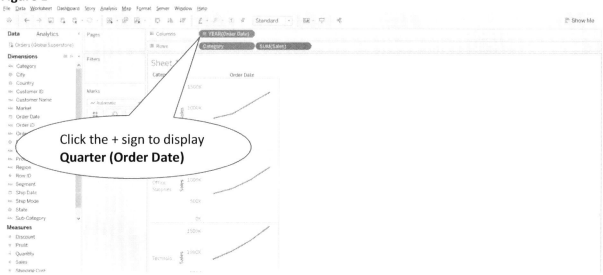

- Click the + sign as shown on Figure 1, which will lead to Figure 2

Figure 2

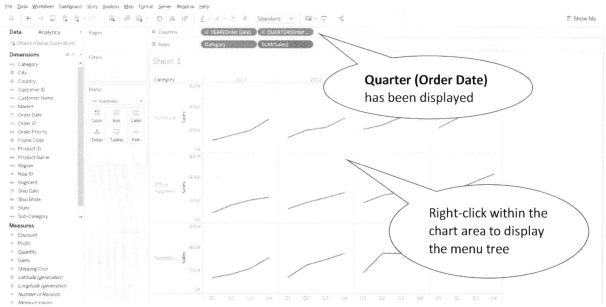

- Right-click within the chart as shown on Figure 2, which will pop-up the menu tree displayed on Figure 3

Figure 3

- Click **Copy** as shown on Figure 3, which will lead to the secondary menu tree displayed on Figure 4

Figure 4

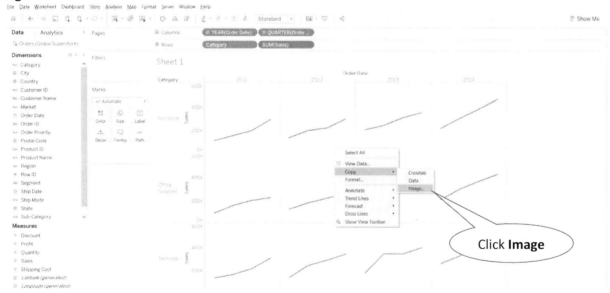

- Click **Image** as shown on Figure 4, which will popup the **Copy Image** window displayed on Figure 5

Figure 5

- Click **Copy** as shown on Figure 5, which will capture the displayed image

The displayed image can now be exported to another application. To export the image into PowerPoint:
- Launch PowerPoint
- Paste onto a blank PowerPoint slide, which will lead to Figure 6 where the image is displayed

Figure 6

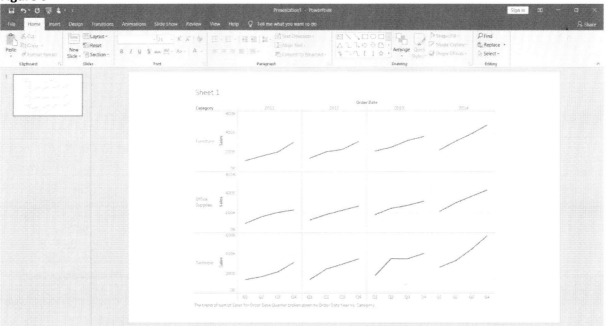

Exercise 24: Export Data

Objective: This exercise will demonstrate how to display and save data associated with a displayed visualization

Note: Use the **Global Superstore** file for this exercise

- Develop the visualization shown on Figure 1

Figure 1

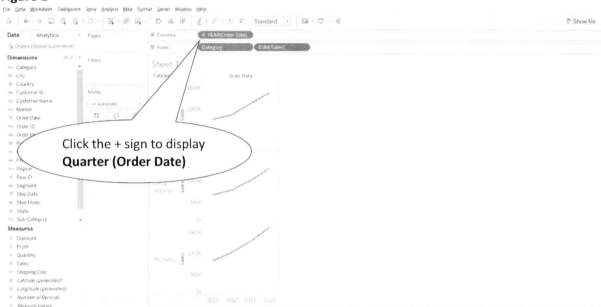

The column row shows order date by year. In order to view the data fpr year and quarter:
- Click the + sign to display **Quarter (Order Date)** as shown on Figure 1, which will lead to Figure 2

Figure 2

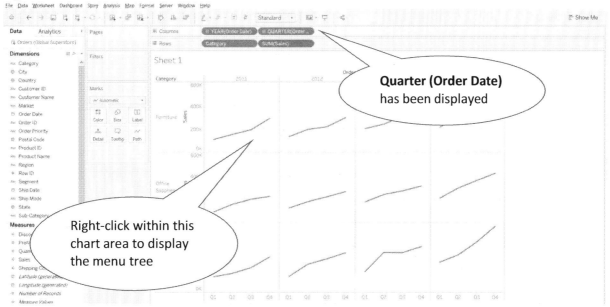

- Right-click within the chart area as shown on Figure 2, which will popup the menu tree displayed on Figure 3

Figure 3

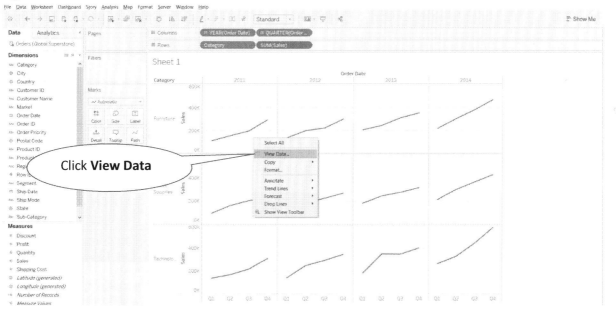

- Click **View Data** as shown on Figure 3, which will popup the **View Data** window displayed on Figure 4

Figure 4

The **View Data** popup window displays the underlying data, which can be analyzed, exported, or saved. To save the data:

- Click the **Export All** button as shown on Figure 4, which will lead to the **Export Data** popup window displayed on Figure 5

Figure 5

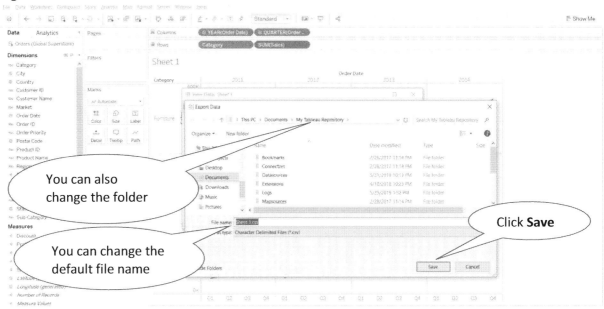

On Figure 5, if desired, you can change the default file name or the default folder (where you want to save the workbook). If/when changes have been made and you are ready to save:

- Click **Save** as shown on Figure 5, which will save the data

Note: On a Mac, Tableau may not provide a default file name

To export data using the Crosstab function:
- Develop the visualization shown in Figure 6 (which is the same as Figure 2)

Figure 6

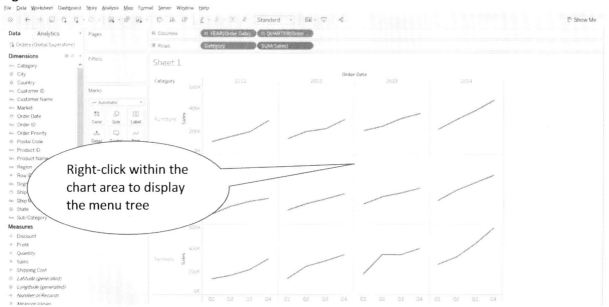

- Right-click within the chart area as shown on Figure 6, which will popup the menu tree displayed on Figure 7

Figure 7

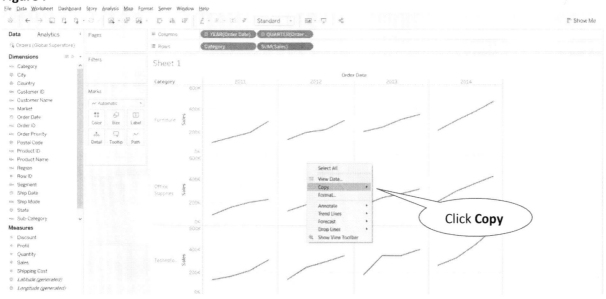

- Click **Copy** as shown on Figure 7, which will display the secondary menu displayed on Figure 8

Figure 8

- Click **Crosstab** as shown on Figure 8, which will capture the data for export

The captured data can now be copied onto an Excel spreadsheet. To copy this data:
- Open a new Excel worksheet (Figure 9)

Figure 9

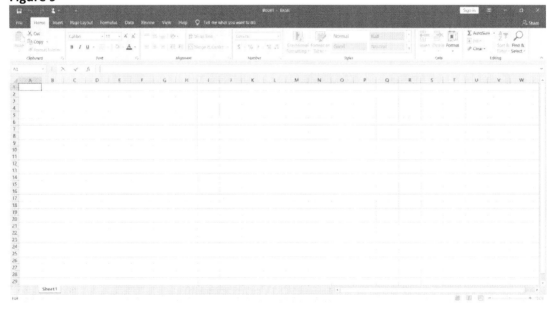

- Paste the data in the open spreadsheet (you can use the Windows Control+V function for this purpose)

The pasted data is displayed on Figure 10.

Figure 10

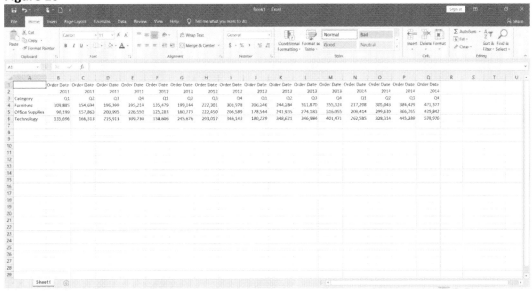

Note: Use the **Sample Superstore** file for the next exercise, which demonstrates an alternative method for exporting crosstab data

- Develop the Figure 11 visualization

Figure 11

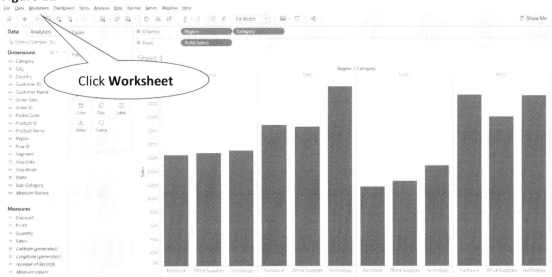

- Click **Worksheet** as shown on Figure 11, which will popup the menu tree displayed on Figure 12

Figure 12

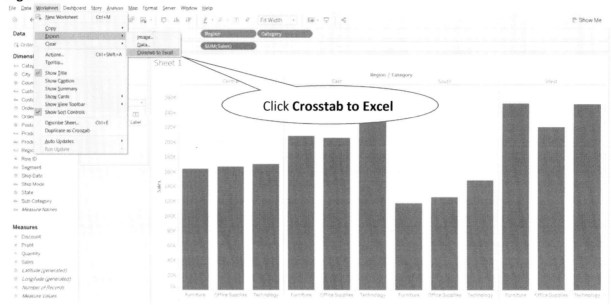

- Navigate as shown on Figure 12 *(Worksheet > Export > Crosstab to Excel)*
- Click the **Crosstab to Excel** menu tree item as shown on Figure 12, which will open an Excel spreadsheet and populate it with the underlying data, as shown on Figure 13

Figure 13

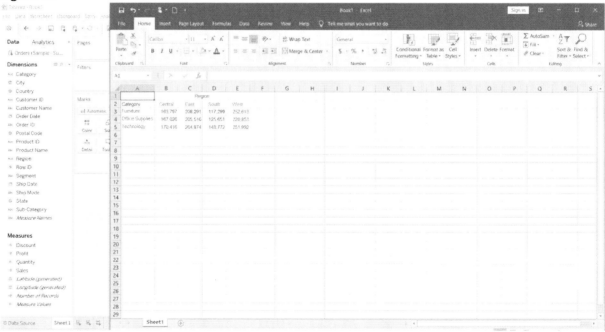

Exercise 25: Display Full Data

Objective: This exercise will demonstrate how to display and export the detailed underlying data behind a visualization

- Develop the Figure 1 visualization, which displays the sum of sales by region by category

Figure 1

- Right-click in the chart area as shown on Figure 1, which will popup the menu tree displayed on Figure 2

Figure 2

- Click **View Data** as shown on Figure 2, which will popup the **View Data** window displayed on Figure 3

Figure 3

To view the detailed data:
- Click the **Full Data** tab as shown on Figure 3, which will lead to Figure 4

Figure 4

To export and save the displayed data:
- Click **Export All** as shown on Figure 4, which will popup the **Export Data** window displayed on Figure 5

Figure 5

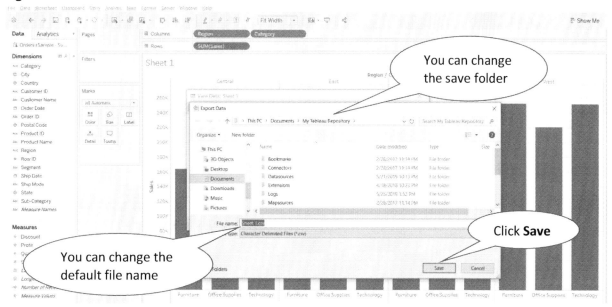

As shown on Figure 5, you can change the folder where you want to save the exported data. If needed, you can also change the default file name.

If changes are required, make the changes as instructed on Figure 5:
- Change the folder name
- Change the file name

To save the exported data:
- Click **Save** as shown on Figure 5

Chapter 6: Formatting

Exercise 26: Formatting

Objective: This exercise will demonstrate commonly used formatting functions

Note: Use the **Sample - Superstore** spreadsheet for this exercise

- Develop the Figure 1 visualization, which will be used to demonstrate basic formatting functions

Figure 1

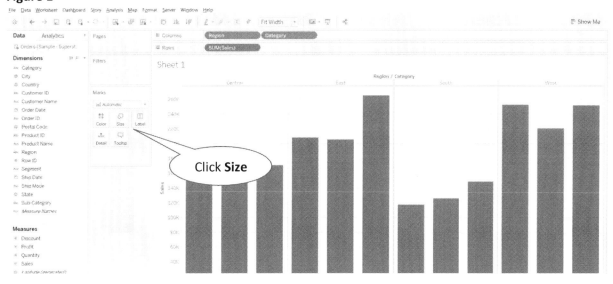

To size the width of the bars:
- Click the **Size** icon on the **Marks Card** as shown on Figure 1, which will lead to Figure 2 where a slider is shown

Figure 2

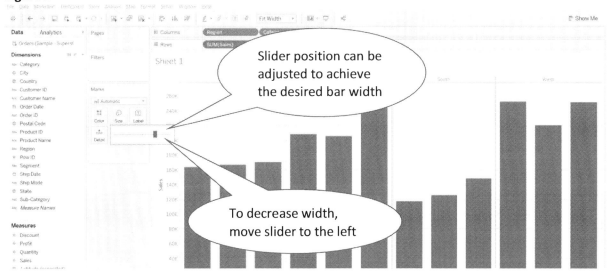

A slider can be used to change the width of a bar simply by adjusting the slider position. To decrease the bar width:

- Move the slider to the left as shown on Figure 2, which will decrease the bar width as shown on Figure 3

Figure 3

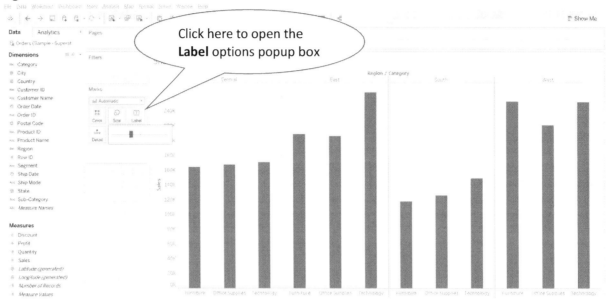

To display the individual values for the bars:

- Click the **Label** icon on the **Marks Card** as shown on Figure 3, which will popup the box displayed on Figure 4

Figure 4

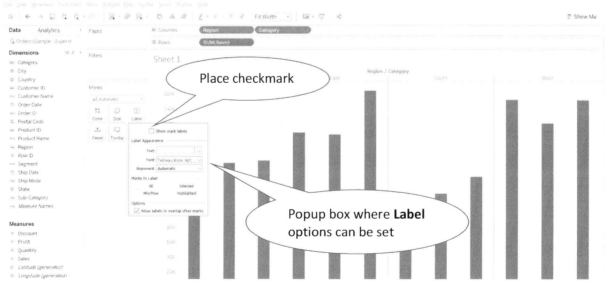

- Place checkmark in the **Show mark labels** field as shown on Figure 4, which will lead to Figure 5

Figure 5

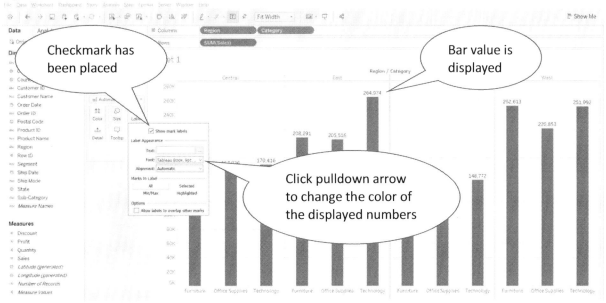

To change the color of the displayed numbers:

- Click the **Font** pulldown arrow as shown on Figure 5

This will popup another box which is shown on Figure 6, where the font size and color can be changed.

Figure 6

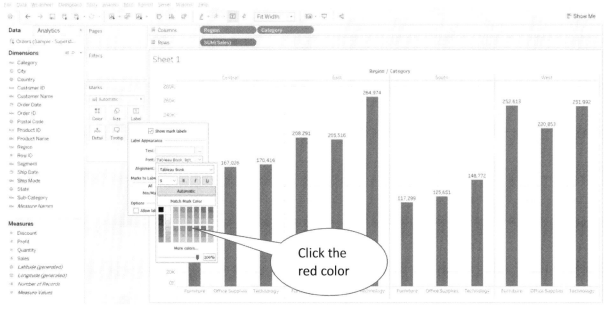

- Click the **Red** color as shown on Figure 6, which will change the color of the displayed numbers to red as shown on Figure 7

Figure 7

- Close the popup boxes by hitting the Esc key twice or clicking outside the popup boxes, which will lead to Figure 8

Figure 8

To change the color of the bars:

- Click the **Color** icon in the **Marks Card** as shown on Figure 8, which will open the **Color** popup box shown on Figure 9

Figure 9

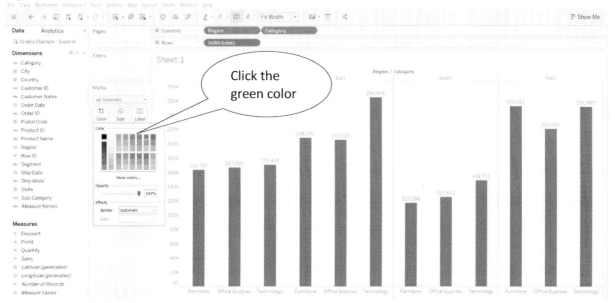

- Click the green color in the **Color** popup box as shown on Figure 9, which will lead to Figure 10 (where the bar colors have changed to green)

Figure 10

To access additional formatting functionality:
- Right-click within the chart area, which will popup the menu tree displayed on Figure 11

Figure 11

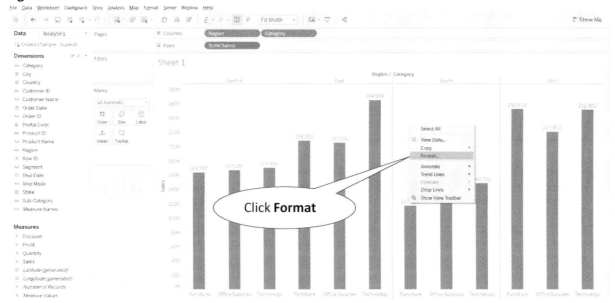

- Click the **Format** menu tree item as shown on Figure 11, which will popup the **Format Font** pane displayed on Figure 12

Figure 12

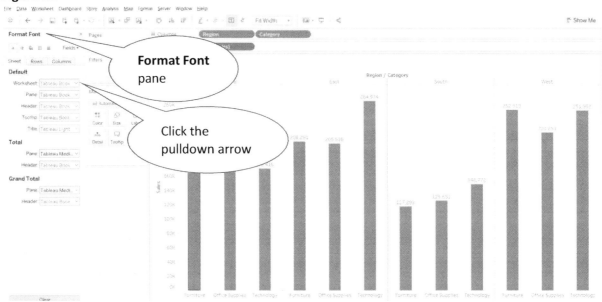

Various formatting operations can now be executed through the **Format Font** pane for the **Sheet**, **Rows** or **Columns** tabs. These can be selected by clicking on the appropriate tab. In Figure 12, the **Sheet** tab has been selected (by default).

- Click the **Worksheet** pulldown arrow as shown on Figure 12, which will popup the box displayed on Figure 13 where the desired changes can be made

Figure 13

- Click the blue color as shown on Figure 13, which will change the color of the column and row titles to blue (as shown on Figure 14)

Figure 14

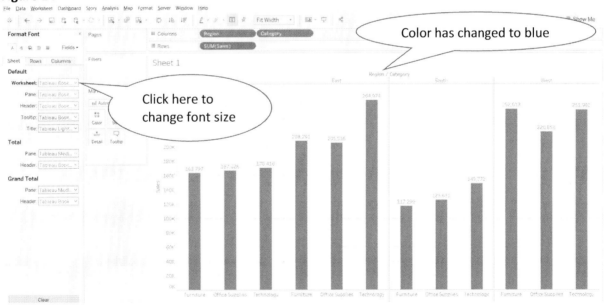

- Click the **Worksheet** pulldown arrow as shown on Figure 14, which will lead to Figure 15

Figure 15

- Click the font size pulldown arrow as shown on Figure 15, which will display the different font sizes as shown on Figure 16

Figure 16

- Click 11 as shown on Figure 16, which will increase the text size to 11 for the row and column headers as shown on Figure 17

Figure 17

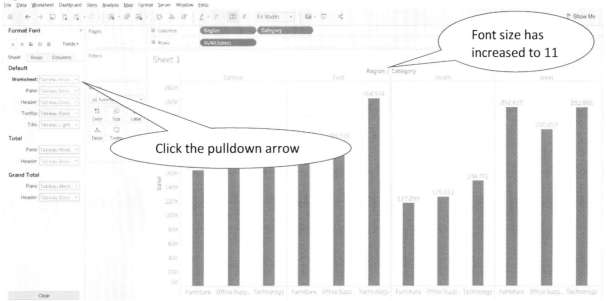

- Click the **Worksheet** pulldown arrow as shown on Figure 17, which will popup the box displayed on Figure 18

Figure 18

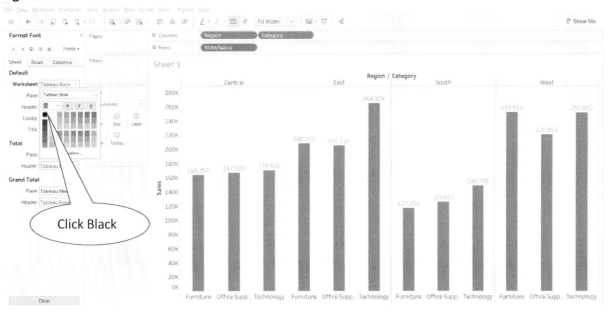

To change the color for the column and row headers to black (from blue):
- Click black in the color selection box as shown on Figure 18, which will lead to Figure 19 (where the headers have changed to black)

Figure 19

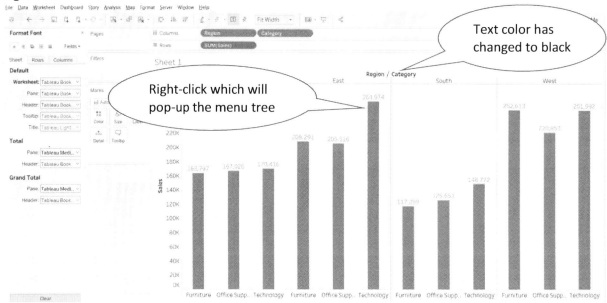

Annotations are text boxes used to highlight a specific mark or point or the entire area of a view. To add an annotation for highlighting a chart:

- Right-click on the bar for the **East** as shown on Figure 19, which will popup the menu tree displayed on Figure 20

Figure 20

- Navigate to **Annotate > Mark** as shown on Figure 20, which will popup up the **Edit Annotation** box displayed on Figure 21

Figure 21

The default annotation can be accepted as-is or it can be modified by typing in the desired text in the **Edit Annotation** box, as shown on Figure 21. In this case, we will not add any custom text.

- Click **OK** as shown on Figure 21, which will add the annotation shown on Figure 21

Figure 21

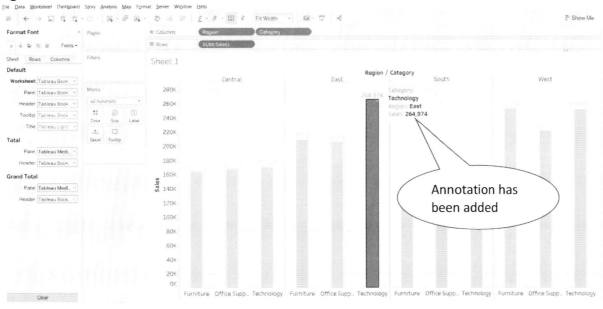

173

Exercise 27: Highlighting with Colors

Objective: This exercise will demonstrate how to highlight the display

Note: Use the **Sample - Superstore** spreadsheet for this exercise

- Develop the visualization on Figure 1 which shows sales by Sub-Category, Year and Quarter

Figure 1

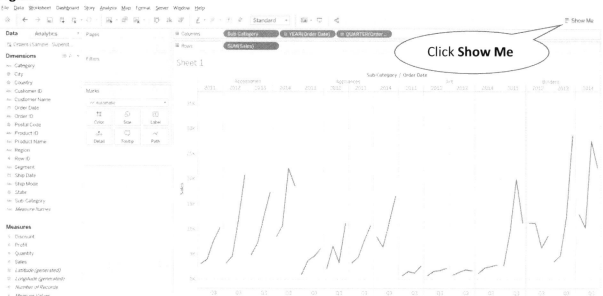

- Click the **Show Me** button as shown on Figure 1, which will lead to Figure 2

Figure 2

- Click the **Text Tables** icon as shown on Figure 2, which will lead to Figure 3 where the data is displayed in table format

Figure 3

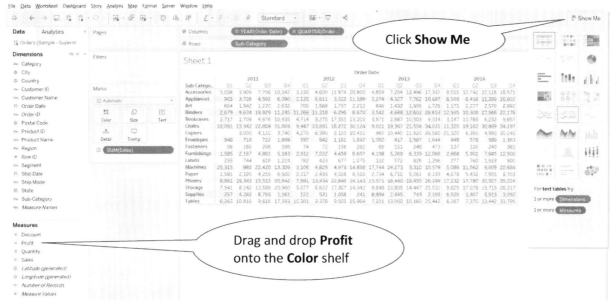

To analyze the profits:
- Click **Show Me** to close the window
- Drag and drop **Profit** onto the **Color** shelf in the **Marks Card** as shown on Figure 3, which will lead to Figure 4

Figure 4

The red and green colors indicate the relative profitability or loss for the relevant item. On this visualization, the displayed colors are not bright and some enhancement is desired.

To enhance the colors:
- Click the **Color** icon in the **Marks Card** as shown on Figure 4, which will popup the window displayed on Figure 5

Figure 5

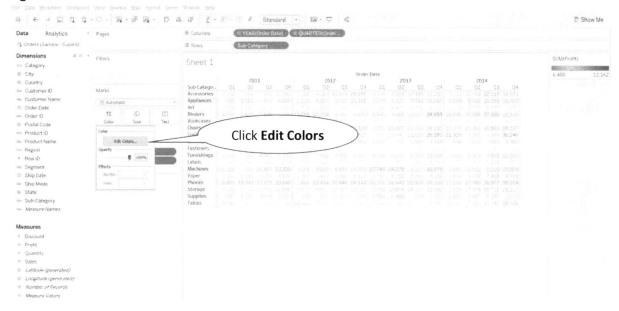

- Click **Edit Colors** icon in the **Marks Card** as shown on Figure 5, which will popup the window displayed on Figure 6

Figure 6

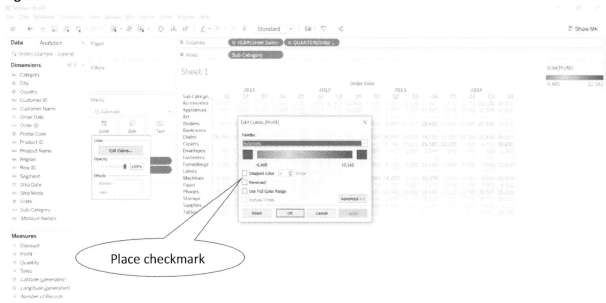

- Place a checkmark in the checkbox located to the left of **Stepped Color** as shown on Figure 6, which will lead to Figure 7

Figure 7

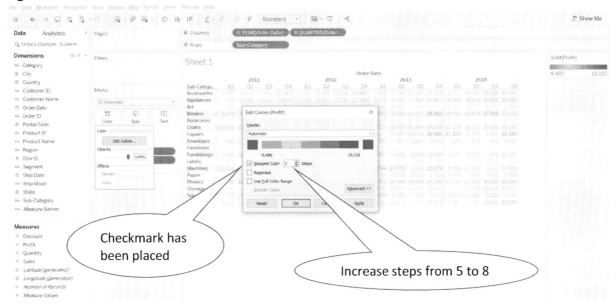

- Increase the **Steps** from 5 to 8, as shown on Figure 7, which will lead to Figure 8

Figure 8

- Click **OK** as shown on Figure 8, which will lead to Figure 9

Figure 9

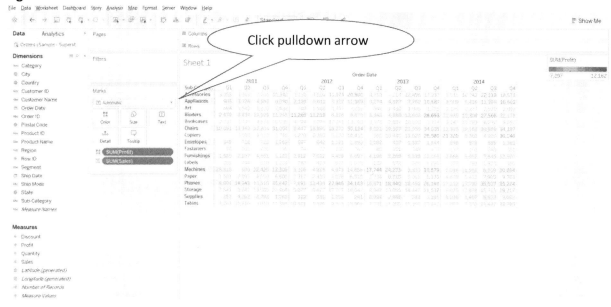

- Click the pulldown arrow for **Automatic** as shown on Figure 9, which will lead to the menu tree displayed on Figure 10

Figure 10

- Click **Square** as shown on Figure 10, which will lead to Figure 11

Figure 11

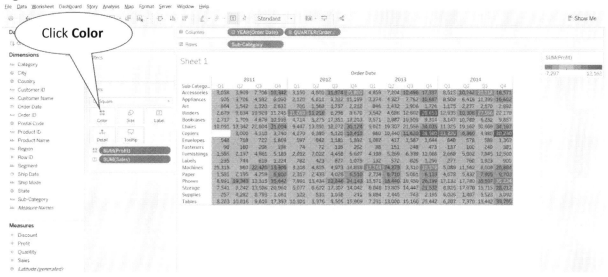

To subdue the colors in the Figure 11 table:

- Click the **Color** icon in the **Marks Card**, which will lead to Figure 12

Figure 12

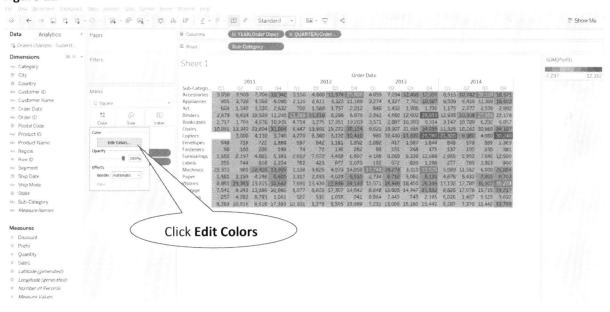

- Click the **Edit Colors** button in the popup window, which will lead to Figure 13

Figure 13

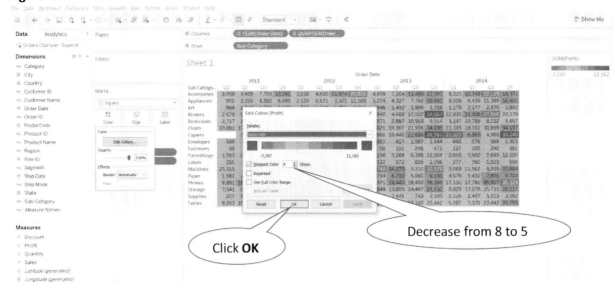

- Change steps from 8 to 5 as shown on Figure 13
- Click **OK** which will lead to Figure 14, where the color intensity has changed

Figure 14

Exercise 28: Axis Formatting

Objective: This exercise will demonstrate how to format the chart axes and display labels

Note: Use the **Global Superstore** file for this exercise

- Develop Figure 1, which displays the plot of the sum of sales for different markets

Figure 1

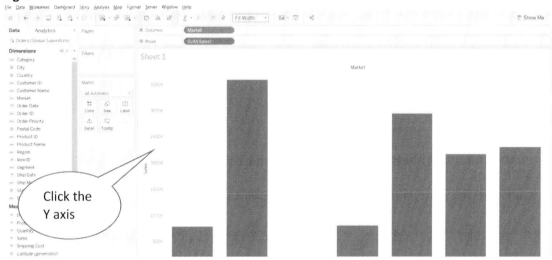

- Click vertical axis as shown on Figure 1, which will lead to Figure 2, where the axis is highlighted

Figure 2

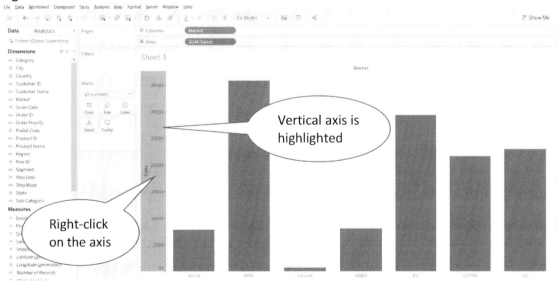

- Right-click Y axis as shown on Figure 2, which will popup the menu tree displayed on Figure 3

Figure 3

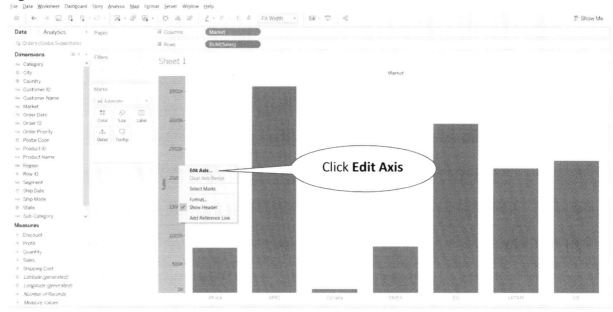

- Click **Edit Axis** as shown on Figure 3, which will popup the **Edit Axis (Profit)** box displayed on Figure 4

Figure 4

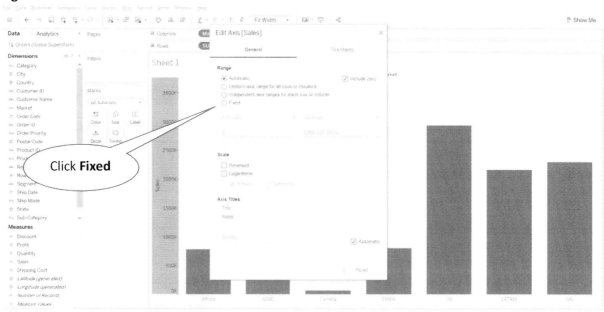

- Click **Fixed** as shown on Figure 4, which will lead to Figure 5

Figure 5

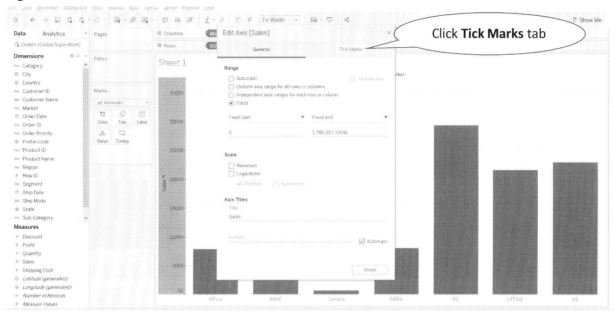

- Click the **Tick Marks** tab as shown on Figure 5, which will lead to Figure 6

Figure 6

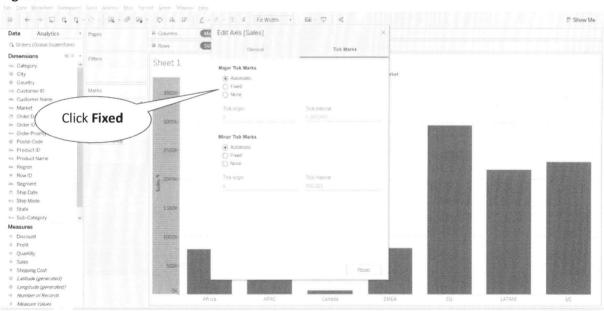

- Click **Fixed** as shown on Figure 6, which will lead to Figure 7

Figure 7

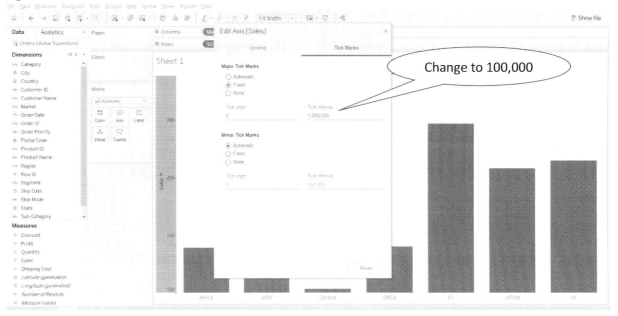

- Change tick interval from 1,000,000 to 100,000 as shown on Figure 7, which will lead to Figure 8

Figure 8

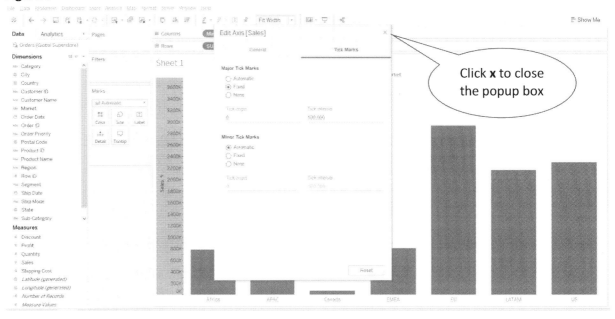

- Click **x** as shown on Figure 8, which will close the **Edit Axis (Sales)** popup box and lead to Figure 9

Figure 9

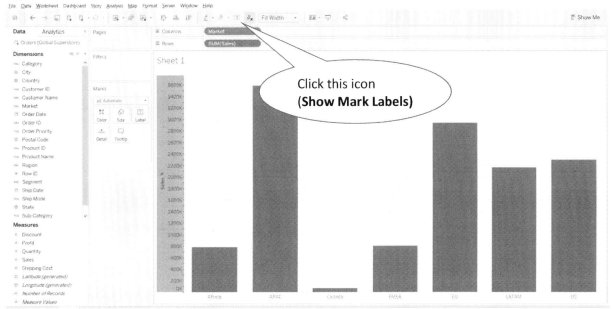

The next part of this exercise demonstrates how to display the values/labels. We will start with Figure 9 which displays a visualization where the numeric values for the individual bars are not displayed.

To view the values for the bars:
- Click the **Show Mark Labels** icon on the Toolbar as shown on Figure 9, which will lead to Figure 10 where the bar values are now displayed

Figure 10

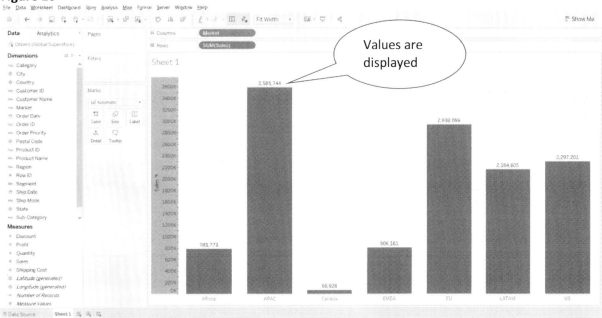

Exercise 29: Formatting Tables

Objective: This exercise will demonstrate how to format a table

Note: Use the **Sample - Superstore** spreadsheet for this exercise

- Develop the visualization displayed on Figure 1

Figure 1

- Click the **Show Me** button as shown on Figure 1, which will lead to Figure 2

Figure 2

- Click the **Text Tables** icon as shown on Figure 2, which will lead to Figure 3

Figure 3

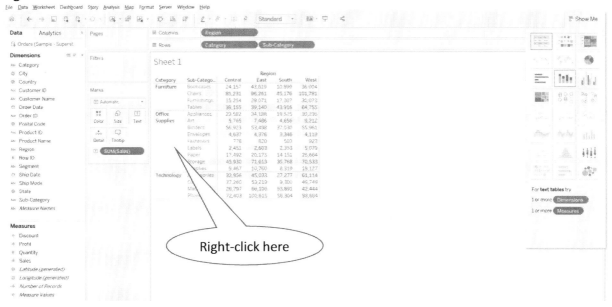

- Right-click the table displayed on Figure 3, which will popup the menu tree shown on Figure 4

Figure 4

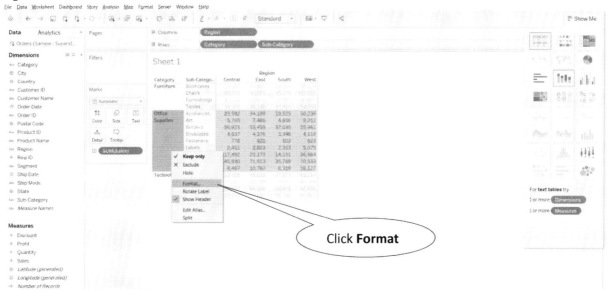

- Click **Format** as shown on Figure 4, which will popup the **Format Category** window displayed on the left-hand side of Figure 5

Figure 5

- Click the **Font** pulldown arrow as shown on Figure 5, which will popup the window displayed on Figure 6

Figure 6

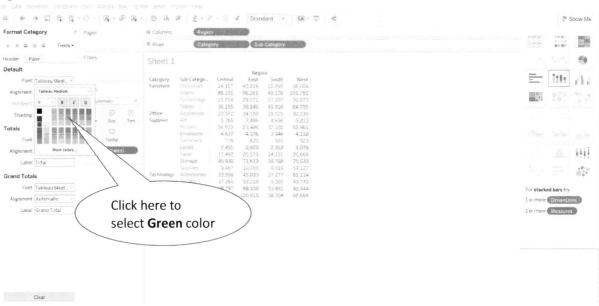

- Click the green color as shown on Figure 6, which will lead to Figure 7 (where the color of the Category header has changed to green)

Figure 7

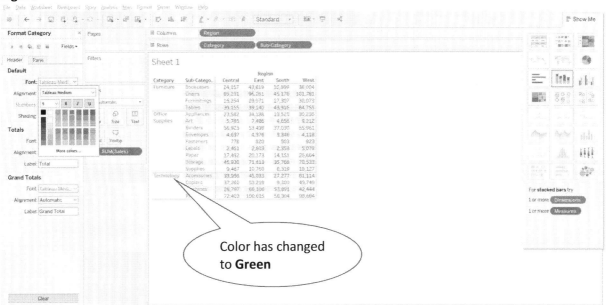

The next procedure will show you how to change the color of the numeric values displayed in a table.

We will start with the table displayed on Figure 8, which is the same as Figure 3. You can develop this visualization by following the steps described earlier (for developing Figures 1-3).

Figure 8

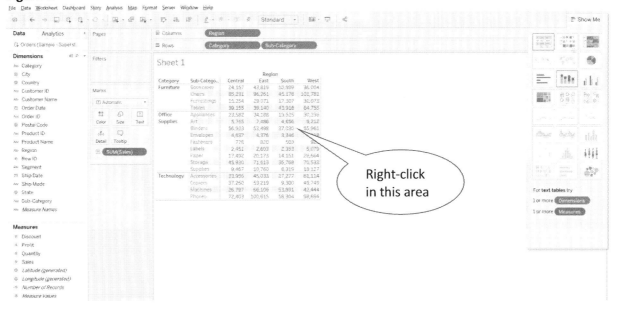

- Right-click in the data area as shown on Figure 8, which will lead to Figure 9

Figure 9

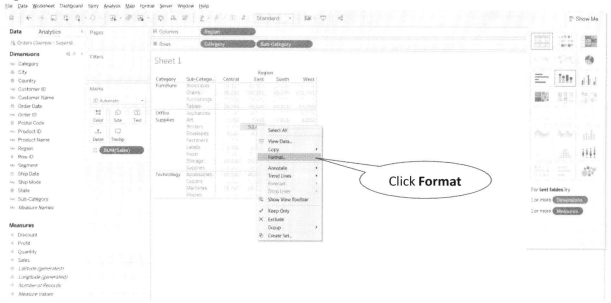

- Click **Format** as shown on Figure 9, which will popup the **Format Font** pane displayed on the left-hand side of the window on Figure 10

Figure 10

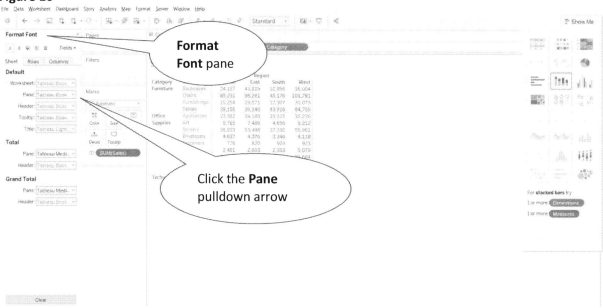

- Click the **Pane** pulldown arrow as shown on Figure 10, which will lead to Figure 11

Figure 11

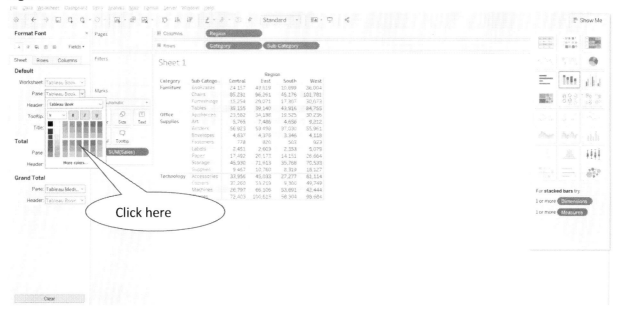

- Click the **Red** color as shown on Figure 11, which will lead to Figure 12 where the numbers are now displayed in red

Figure 12

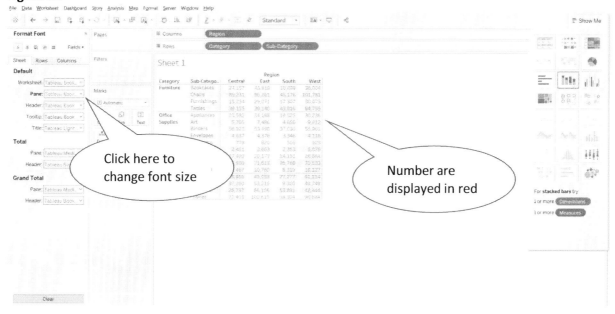

To change the font size:
- Click the **Pane** pulldown arrow as shown on Figure 12, which will lead to Figure 13

Figure 13

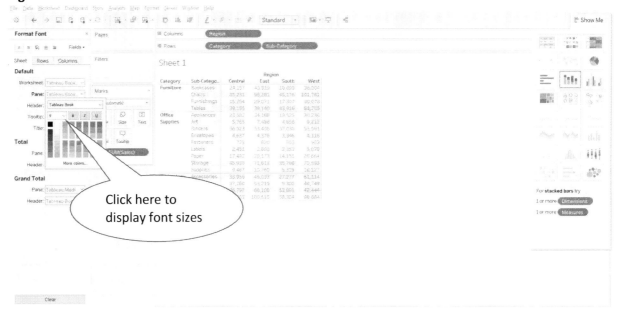

- Click the pulldown arrow as shown on Figure 13, which will lead to Figure 14 where the font size can be selected

Figure 14

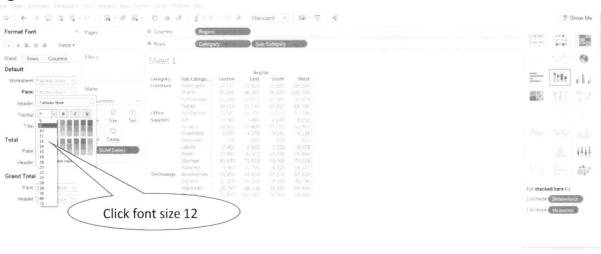

- Click font size 12 as shown on Figure 14, which will lead to Figure 15

Figure 15

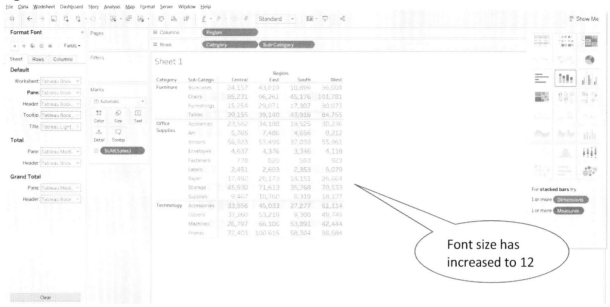

The following steps will demonstrate how to change the column header colors.

- Develop the visualization displayed on Figure 16, using the **Sample – Superstore** spreadsheet

Figure 16

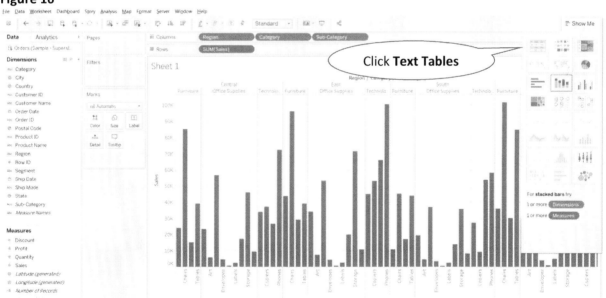

- Click the **Text Tables** icon as shown on Figure 16, which will lead to Figure 17

Figure 17

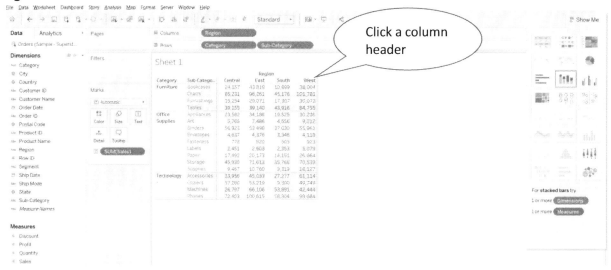

- Click a column header as shown on Figure 17, which will lead to Figure 18

Figure 18

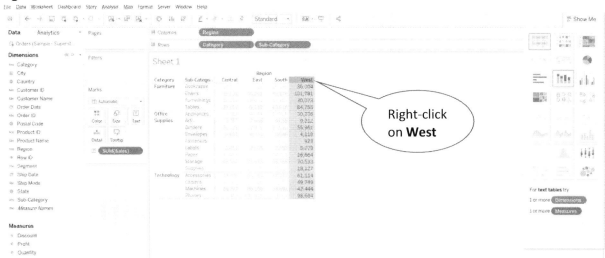

- Right-click on the header **West** as shown on Figure 18, which will popup the menu tree displayed on Figure 19

Figure 19

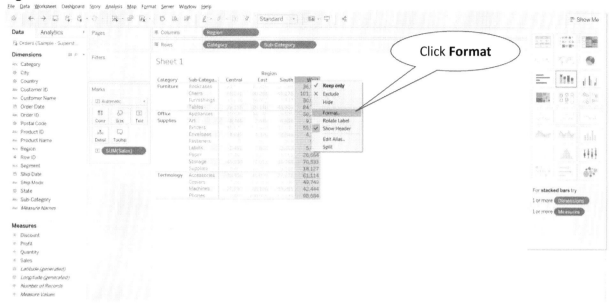

- Click **Format** which will lead to Figure 20, where the **Format Region** pane has popped up

Figure 20

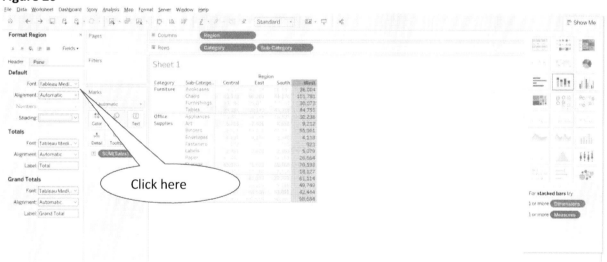

- Click the pulldown arrow as shown on Figure 20, which will lead to Figure 21

Figure 21

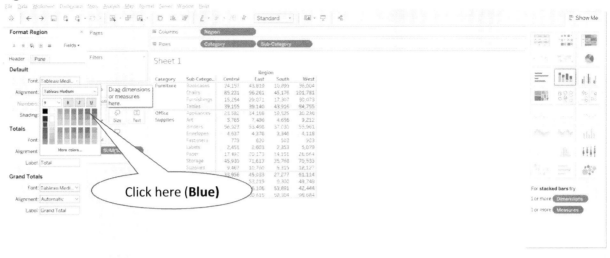

- Click the **Blue** color as shown on Figure 21, which will lead to Figure 22 where the column header color has changed to blue

Figure 22

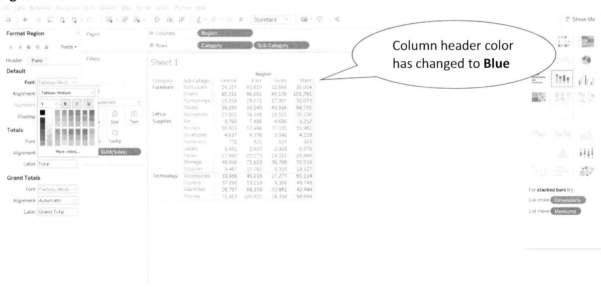

Chapter 7: More functions

Exercise 30: Top N

Objective: This exercise will demonstrate how to use the Top N function

Note: Use the **Sample - Superstore** spreadsheet for this exercise

- Develop Figure 1, which shows a chart with the sum of sales by state

Figure 1

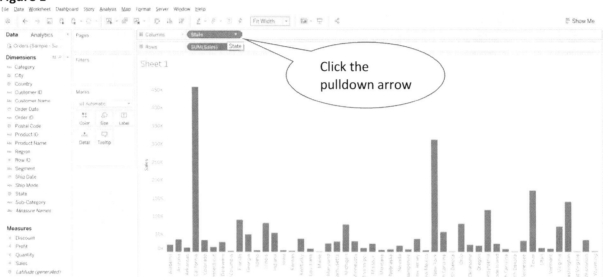

- Click the pulldown arrow for **State** as shown on Figure 1, which will popup the menu tree displayed on Figure 2

Figure 2

- Click **Filter** as shown on Figure 2, which will lead to the **Filter (State)** popup window displayed on Figure 3

Figure 3

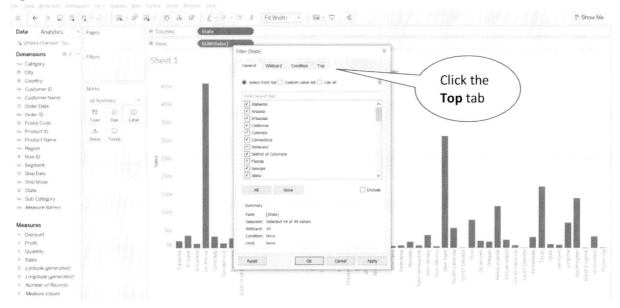

- Click the **Top** tab as shown on Figure 3, which will lead to the popup window shown on Figure 4

Figure 4

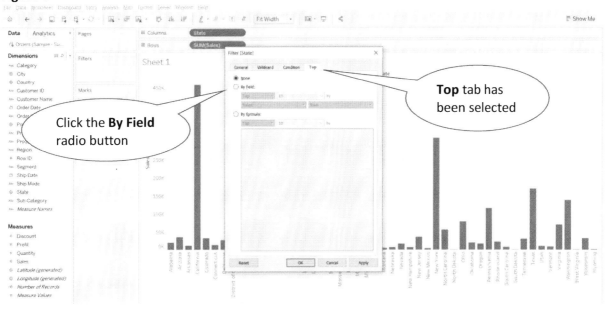

- Click the **By Field** radio button as shown on Figure 4, which will lead to the display on Figure 5

Figure 5

- Click **OK** as shown on Figure 5, which will lead to Figure 6 where the 10 top states with the highest sales are displayed

Figure 6

To view the top ten states by profit, rather than by sales:
- Click **State** as shown on Figure 6, which will display its pulldown arrow

When the pulldown arrow is displayed:
- Click on it, which will lead to Figure 7 where the menu tree is displayed

Figure 7

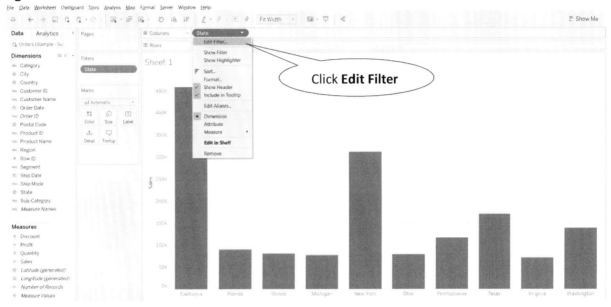

- Click **Edit Filter** as shown on Figure 7, which will lead to Figure 8

Figure 8

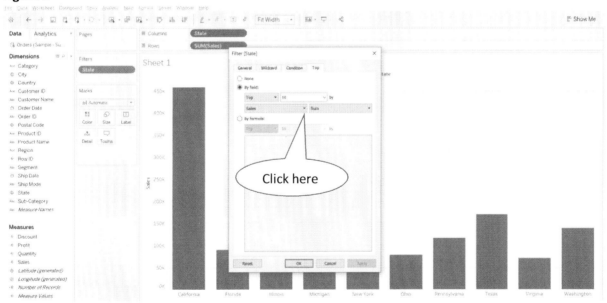

- Click the pulldown arrow for **Sales** as shown on Figure 8, which will lead to the menu tree displayed on Figure 9 (from which the desired field, **Profit**, can be selected)

Figure 9

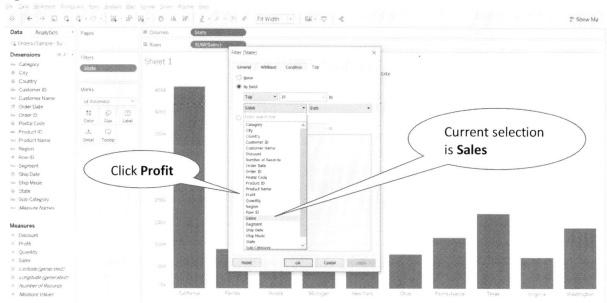

The current selection is **Sales** as shown on Figure 9. To change it to **Profit**:
- Click **Profit** as shown on Figure 9, which will lead to Figure 10

Figure 10

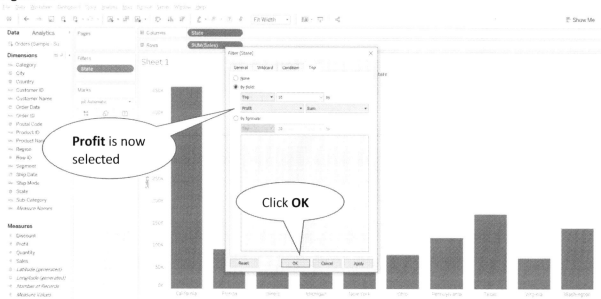

- Click **OK** as shown on Figure 10, which will lead to Figure 11 where the 10 top states with the highest profit are displayed

Figure 11

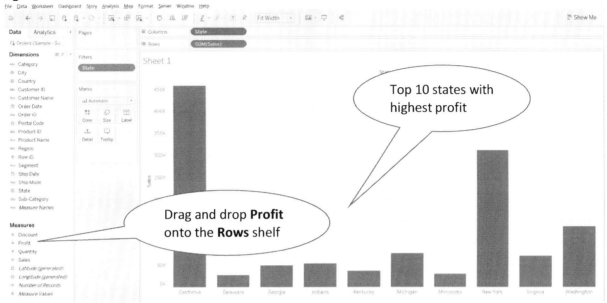

Figure 11 displays **Sales** on the vertical axis. To simultaneously view **Profit** on the vertical axis:
- Drag and drop **Profit** onto the **Rows** shelf as shown on Figure 11, which will lead to Figure 12 where both the **Sales and Profits** charts are displayed

Figure 12

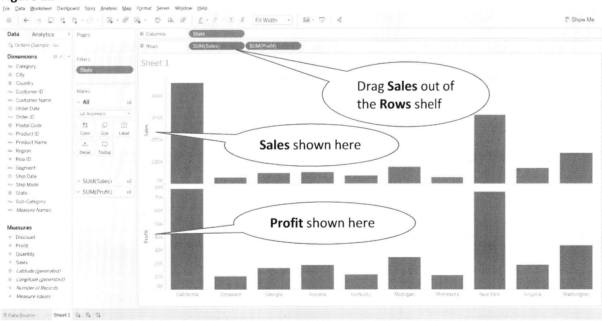

To display **Profit** only on the vertical axis:
- Drag **Sales** out of the **Rows** shelf as shown on Figure 12, which will lead to Figure 13 where only **Profit** is displayed on the vertical axis

Figure 13

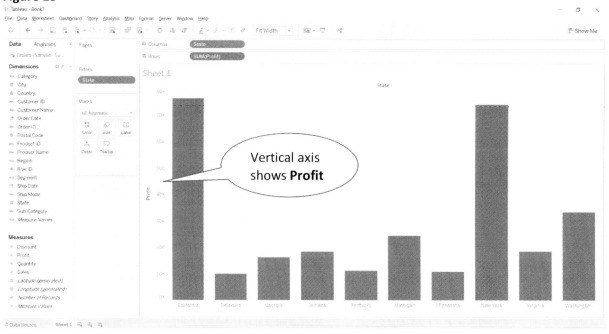

Exercise 31: Trendlines

Objective: This exercise will demonstrate how trendlines can be inserted in a chart

Note: Use the **Global Superstore** file for this exercise

- Develop Figure 1, which displays a line chart showing the sum of sales over a 12-month period

Figure 1

To show a trend line for the displayed data:
- Right-click within the chart area as shown on Figure 1, which will popup the menu tree displayed on Figure 2

Figure 2

- Navigate *Trend Lines > Show Trend Lines* as shown on Figure 2
- Click **Show Trend Lines** as shown on Figure 2, which will lead to Figure 3 where the trend line has been inserted

Figure 3

- Hover over the trend line as shown on Figure 3, which will display more information about the trend such as P-value (as shown on Figure 4)

Figure 4

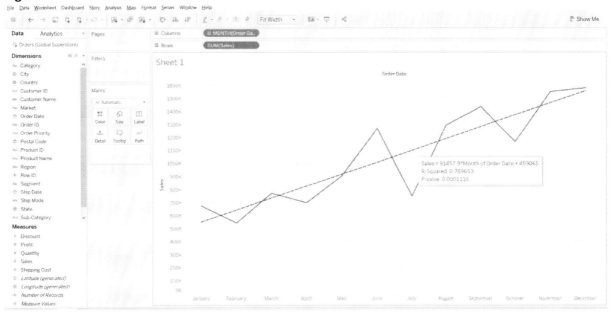

Figure 4 displays the P-value which indicates the significance of the results. A smaller value indicates that the results are significant. However, a large P-value can indicate that the trend in the data is due to chance—not due to the model.

An alternative method can also be used for inserting trend lines in a chart, which is demonstrated in the following steps. For this method, we will start with the visualization displayed on Figure 5.

Figure 5

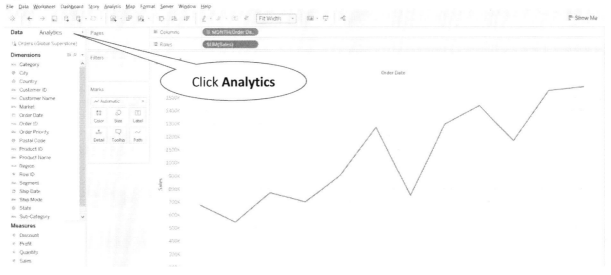

- Click the **Analytics** tab in the **Data Window** as shown on Figure 5, which will lead to the display on Figure 6

Figure 6

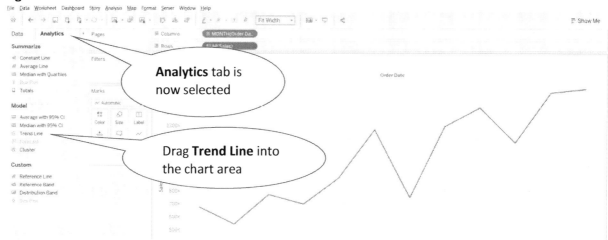

- Drag **Trend Line** into the chart area as shown on Figure 6, which will popup the box displayed on Figure 7

Figure 7

The desired type of trend line can be selected on the popup box. To select the exponential model:
- Drop the dragged item, *Trend Line*, onto the **Exponential** icon as shown on Figure 7, which will generate the trend line displayed on Figure 8

Figure 8

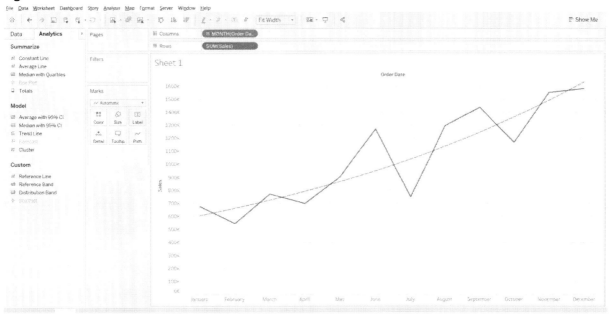

Exercise 32: Forecasting

Objective: This exercise will demonstrate the forecasting feature in Tableau

Note: Use the **Sample - Superstore** spreadsheet for this exercise

- Develop the Figure 1 visualization, which shows the sales by year, quarter and month

Figure 1

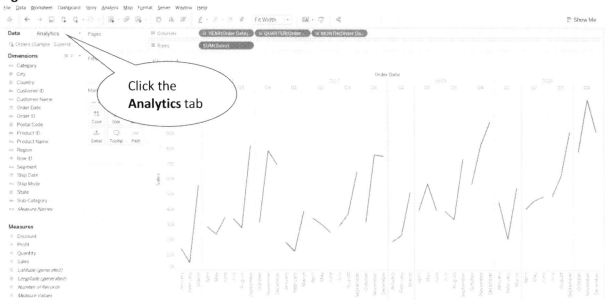

- Click the **Analytics** tab as shown on Figure 1, which will lead to Figure 2

Figure 2

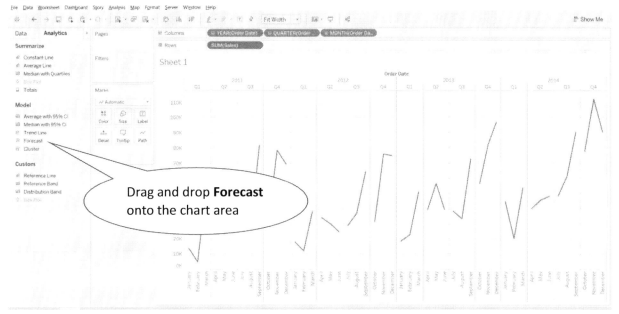

- Drag and drop **Forecast** from the **Analytics** tab onto the chart area as shown on Figure 2, which will lead to Figure 3 where the forecast is displayed

Figure 3

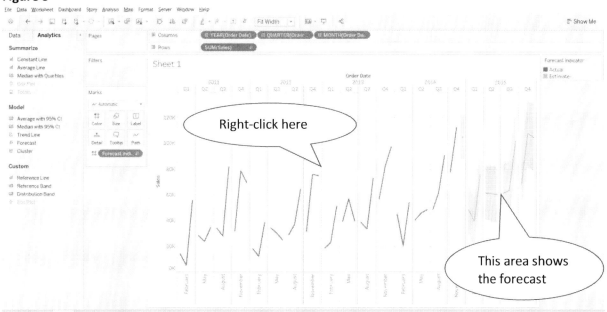

- Right-click in the chart area as shown on Figure 3, which will popup the menu tree displayed on Figure 4

Figure 4

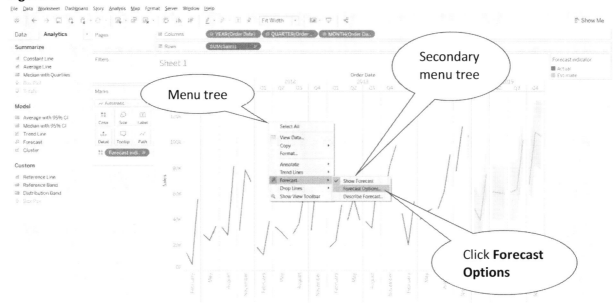

- Navigate to the **Forecast** secondary menu tree as shown on Figure 4
- Click **Forecast Options** as shown on Figure 4, which will popup the **Forecast Options** window displayed on Figure 5

Figure 5

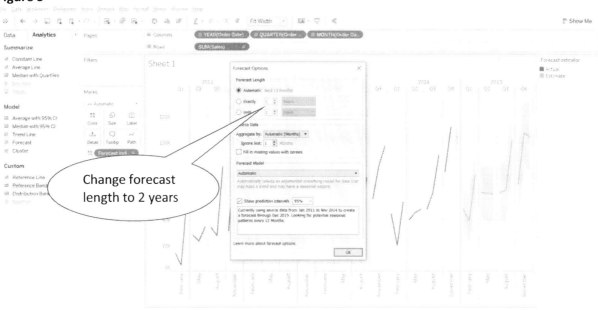

- Change the **Forecast Length** to 2 years as shown on Figure 5, which will lead to Figure 6

Figure 6

- Click **OK** which will lead to Figure 7, where the forecast for two years is displayed

Figure 7

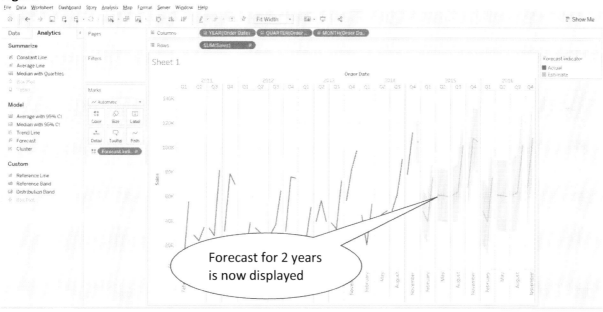

Chapter 8: Dashboards

Exercise 33: Creating a Dashboard

Objective: This exercise will demonstrate how to create a dashboard

Dashboards can be used to present one or more visualizations so that a consolidated view can be provided. A view incorporated into a dashboard is just a window to the underlying worksheet. Dashboards tie different views together and are frequently provided with filters, legends, and interactivity. They can include worksheets, images, texts, as well as webpages. Stories are walkthroughs of one or more dashboards or sheets. While dashboards answer the question "What," stories answer the question "Why."

For this exercise, you will need five worksheets that use the **Global Superstore** spreadsheet.

To start this exercise, develop the following worksheets:
- Sales by Region (sheet 1)
- Sales by Category (sheet 2)
- Profit by Category (sheet 3)
- Sales by Order Date (sheet 4)
- Sales and Profits by Region (sheet 5)

Figure 1 shows what the workbook will look like after the five worksheets have been developed and renamed (Sheet 1 through Sheet 5).

Figure 1

- Click the **New Dashboard** icon as shown on Figure 1, which will lead to Figure 2 where a new dashboard sheet (**Dashboard 1**) has been added

215

Figure 2

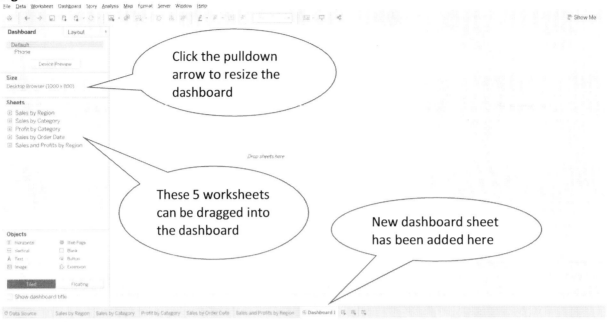

To resize the dashboard display:
- Click the **Size** pulldown arrow as shown on Figure 2, which will popup the menu tree displayed on Figure 3

Figure 3

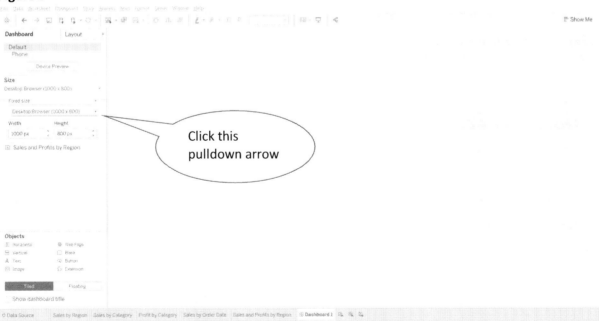

To view the options for resizing:

- Click the **Desktop Browser (1000 x 800)** pulldown arrow as shown on Figure 3, which will popup the menu tree shown on Figure 4

Figure 4

The size to be selected will depend on the device(s) to be used for viewing the dashboard, which can include desktops, laptops, tablets, and smartphones.

In this exercise, we will not change the default display (Desktop Browser). Therefore, we will start with Figure 5 (which is the same as Figure 2).

Figure 5

- Drag and drop the **Sales by Region** sheet onto the Dashboard canvas as shown on Figure 5, which will lead to Figure 6

Figure 6

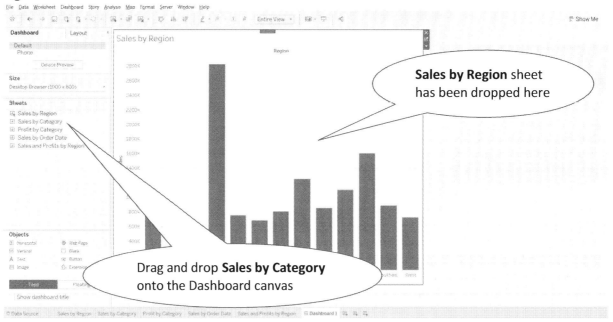

Sales by Region sheet has been dropped here

Drag and drop **Sales by Category** onto the Dashboard canvas

When the first view is brought into a dashboard, it automatically takes up the whole view. However, any subsequent worksheet can be placed in a specific area of the screen. If the mouse button is held down as it is moved around the dashboard, grey areas will indicate where the dragged view will be located when it is let go. If it is brought all the way down to the bottom of the screen, it will fill the entire width.

- Drag and drop the **Sales by Category** worksheet onto the Dashboard area as shown on Figure 6, which will lead to Figure 7

Figure 7

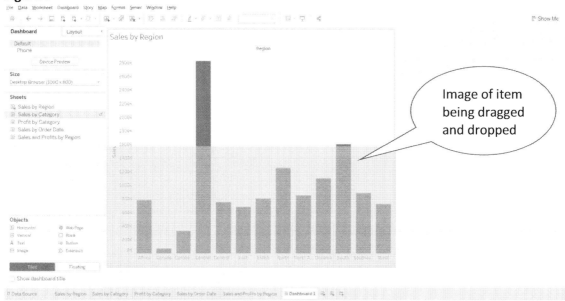

Image of item being dragged and dropped

218

The Figure 7 display occurs when the worksheet is dragged to the dashboard just BEFORE it is dropped. The shaded area indicates the place where the dragged worksheet will be located when it is dropped. You can use the cursor to move the image around till you are satisfied (when you can drop the worksheet).

After the image has been moved to the desired location:
- Drop the **Sales by Category** worksheet onto the Dashboard area as shown on Figure 7, which will lead to Figure 8

Figure 8

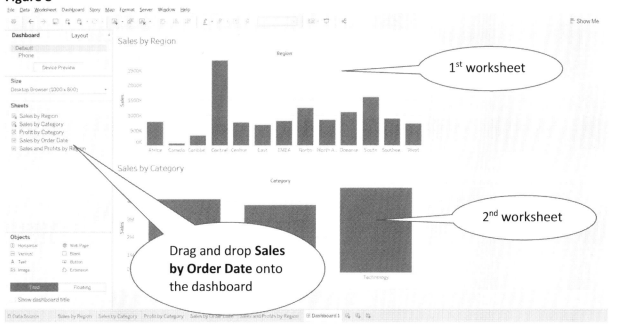

- Drag and drop the **Sales by Order Date** sheet onto the Dashboard area, which will lead to Figure 9

Figure 9

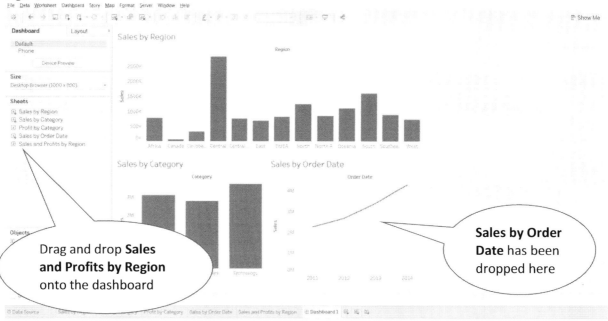

- Drag and drop the **Sales and Profits by Region** worksheet onto the dashboard area as shown on Figure 9, which will lead to Figure 10

Figure 10

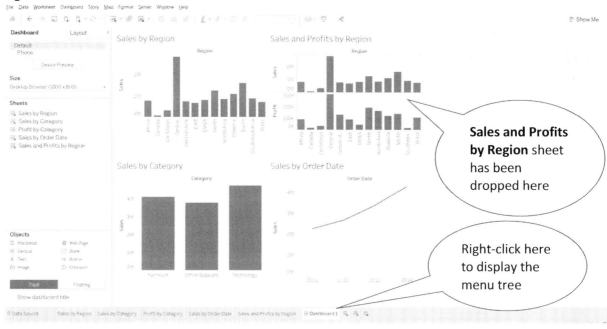

- Right-click on the **Dashboard 1** sheet as shown on Figure 10, which will lead to the menu tree displayed on Figure 11

Figure 11

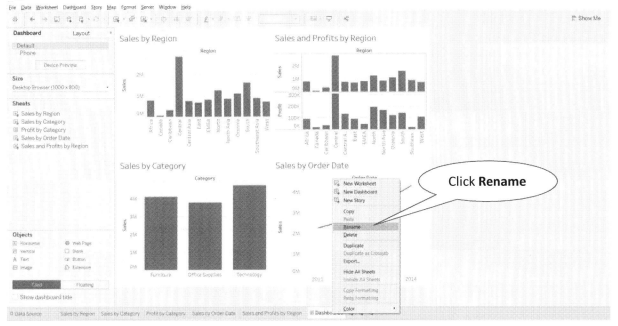

- Click the **Rename** menu tree item as shown on Figure 11, which will lead to Figure 12 where the **Dashboard 1** name is highlighted and can be renamed (Note that the sheet can also be renamed by double-clicking on it and then typing in the new name)

Figure 12

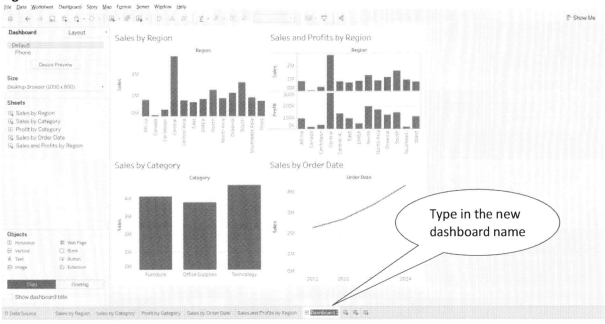

- Rename **Dashboard 1** as **Sales Dashboard**, which will lead to the display on Figure 13, where the new dashboard name is displayed (**Sales Dashboard**)

Figure 13

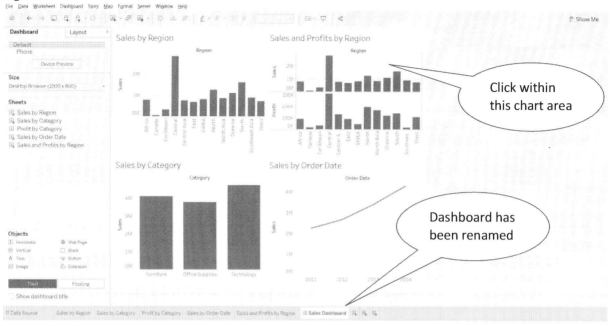

Save this workbook as "**Sales Dashboard**." You will need this workbook for exercises 34 and 35.

The individual worksheets on a dashboard as well as the dashboard itself are customizable. Clicking on a worksheet will display a pulldown arrow, through which various options can be accessed.

To customize the **Sales and Profits by Region** worksheet in the dashboard:
- Click within the **Sales and Profits by Region** window as shown on Figure 13, which will lead to Figure 14 where the chart's pulldown arrow is displayed

Figure 14

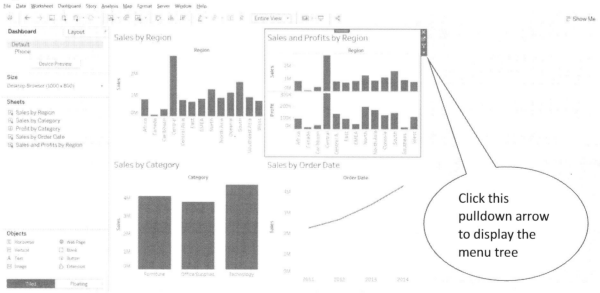

- Click **Sales and Profits by Region's** pulldown arrow as shown on Figure 14, which will lead to the menu tree displayed on Figure 15

Figure 15

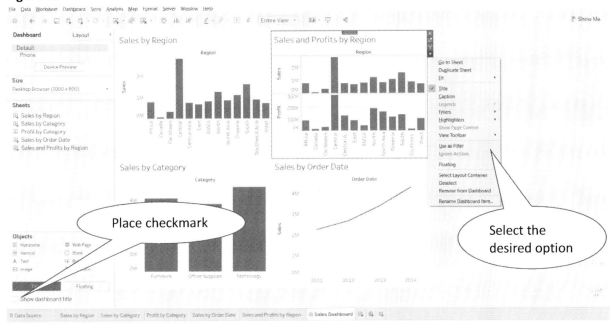

As the menu tree items indicate, there are many options that can be used to customize the sheet, such as displaying the dashboard title (which is not displayed on Figure 15).

To display the dashboard name in the title:
- Place checkmark next to **Show Dashboard Title** as shown on Figure 15, which will lead to Figure 16

Figure 16

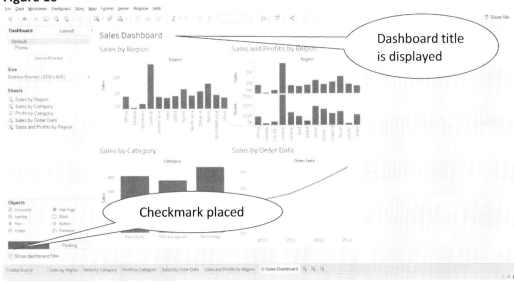

Dashboard items can be rearranged and/or resized as desired. Figure 17 shows the new **Sales Dashboard** layout after the worksheets were rearranged though simple drag and drop operations.

Figure 17

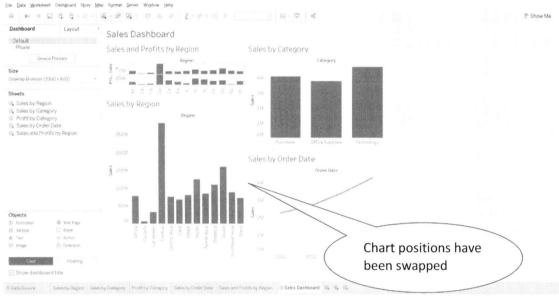

Exercise 34: Dashboard Quick Filters

Objective: This exercise will demonstrate how to apply quick filters for selected worksheets on a dashboard

We will start with the dashboard that was developed in Exercise 33 (*Sales Dashboard*), which is displayed on Figure 1.

Figure 1

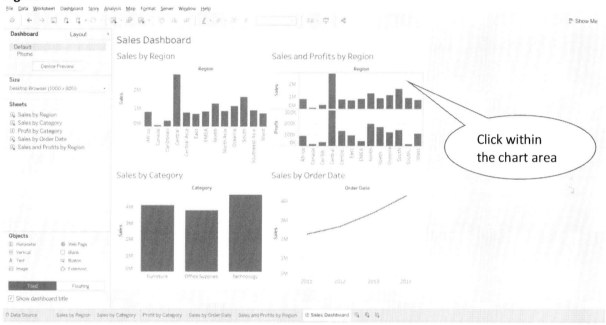

To remove the **Sales and Profits by Region** worksheet from the dashboard:

- Click within the chart area as shown on Figure 1, which will lead to Figure 2

Figure 2

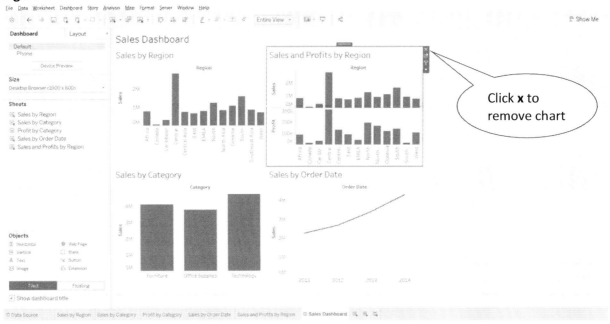

- Click **x** as shown on Figure 2, which will lead to Figure 3 where the chart has been removed from the dashboard

Figure 3

- Click the **Sales and Profits by Region** worksheet as shown on Figure 3, which will lead to Figure 4

Figure 4

To display the **Market** filter:

- Right-click the **Market** dimension as shown on Figure 4, which will lead to Figure 5

Figure 5

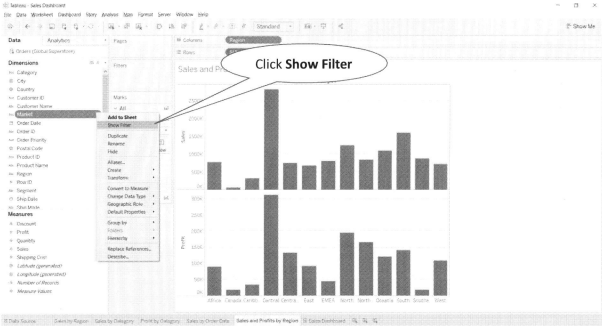

- Click **Show Filter** as shown on Figure 5, which will lead to Figure 6

Figure 6

- Click on **Sales Dashboard** as shown on Figure 6, which will lead to Figure 7

Figure 7

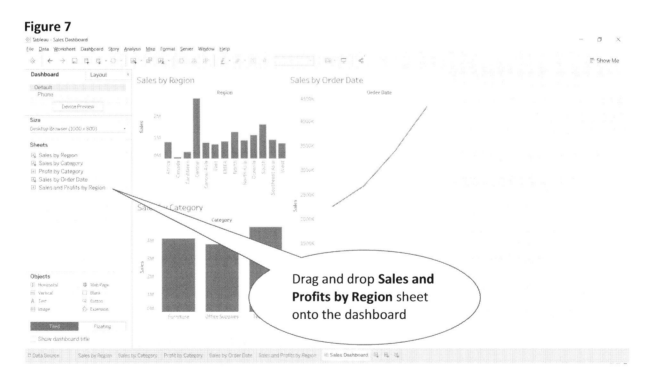

- Drag and drop the **Sales and Profits by Region** sheet onto the dashboard area as shown on Figure 7, which will lead to Figure 8

Figure 8

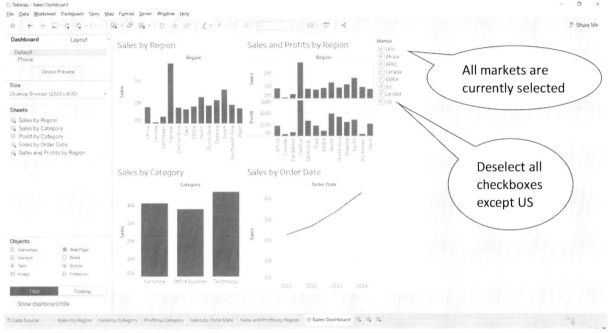

- Deselect all checkboxes except **US** as shown on Figure 8, which will lead to Figure 9 where the data has been restricted to the **US** market

Figure 9

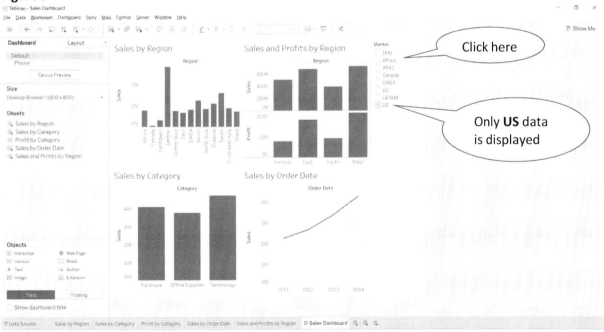

Notice that the other two charts did not change. They still display data for all the markets—not just the US.

- Click in the **Market Quick Filter** area as shown on Figure 9, which will lead to Figure 10, where the filter's pulldown arrow is displayed

Figure 10

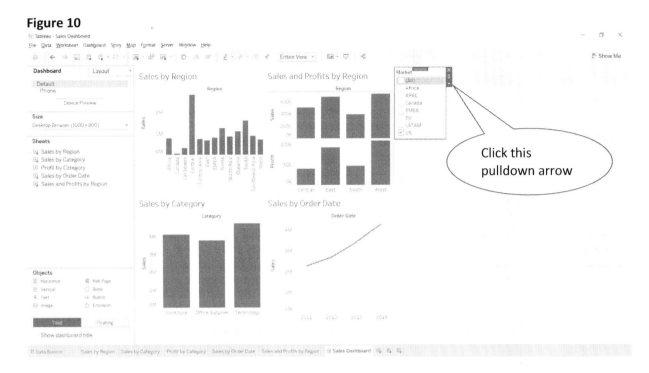

- Click **Market Quick Filter's** pulldown arrow as shown on Figure 10, which will lead to Figure 11

Figure 11

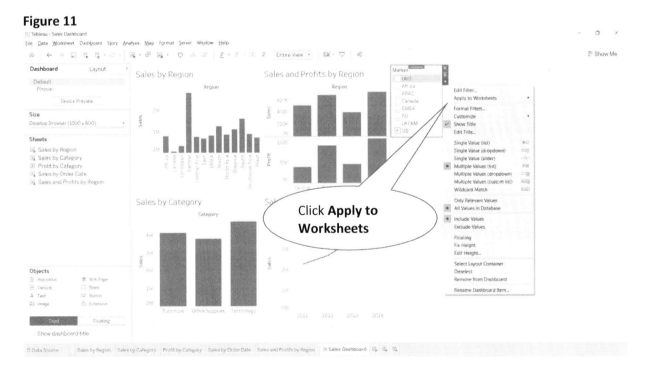

- Click **Apply to Worksheets** as shown on Figure 11, which will lead to Figure 12

Figure 12

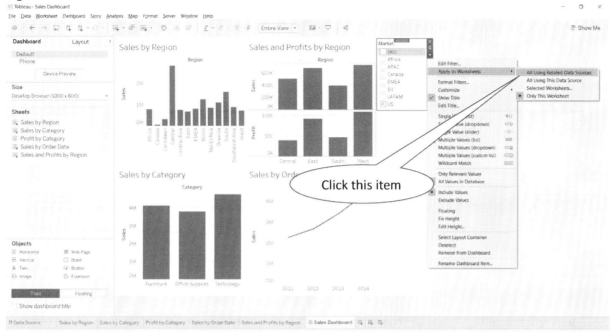

- Click **All Using Related Data Sources** as shown on Figure 12, which will lead to Figure 13 where all three charts now display data for only the US market

Figure 13

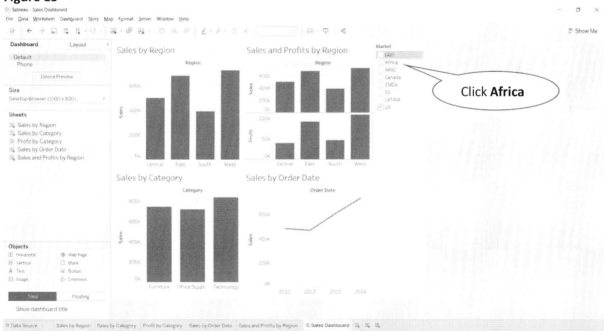

To add another region to the existing filter:

- Click the **Africa** checkbox as shown on Figure 13, which will lead to Figure 14 where the data is displayed for the US as well as Africa

231

Figure 14

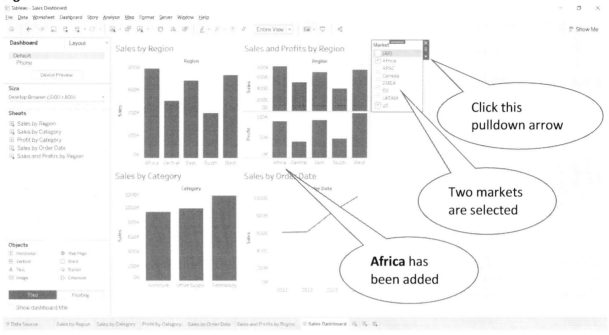

The application of a filter can be made selective. In other words, you can pick and choose the sheets to which a filter can apply.

- Click the pulldown arrow as shown on Figure 14, which will lead to Figure 15

Figure 15

- Click **Apply to Worksheets** as shown on Figure 15, which will lead to Figure 16 where the secondary menu tree is displayed

Figure 16

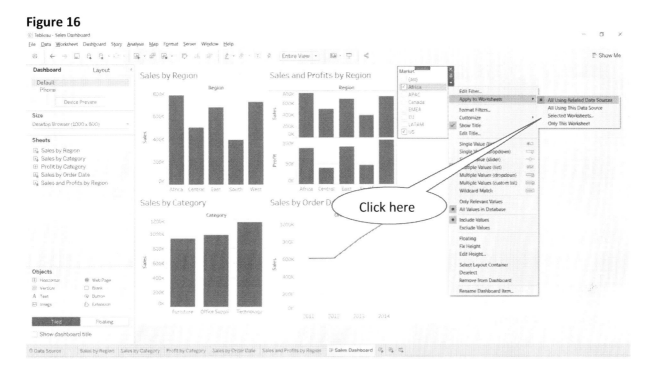

- Click **Selected Worksheets** as shown on Figure 16, which will lead to Figure 17

Figure 17

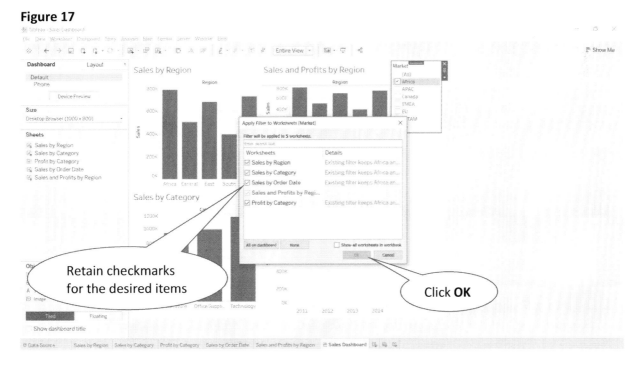

By default, all the dashboard worksheets where the filter can be applied are displayed, as shown on Figure 17. You can pick and choose the worksheets where you want the filter to apply.

To de-select a worksheet:
- Remove the checkmark to the left of the worksheet where you do not want the filter to be applied
- Click **OK** after making the desired changes, which will apply the filter to the remaining worksheet(s)

Exercise 35: Dashboard Layout Formatting

Objective: This exercise will demonstrate how to modify a dashboard's display through layout and formatting changes

We will start with the dashboard that was developed in Exercise 33 (***Sales Dashboard***), which is displayed on Figure 1.

Figure 1

To format the dashboard:

- Click **Format** on the **Menu Bar** as shown on Figure 1, which will popup the menu tree displayed on Figure 2

Figure 2

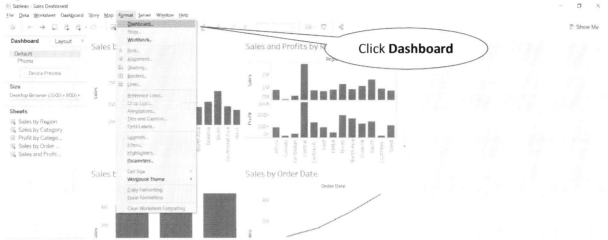

- Click **Dashboard** as shown on Figure 2, which will popup the **Format Dashboard** pane displayed on Figure 3 (on the left-hand side)

Figure 3

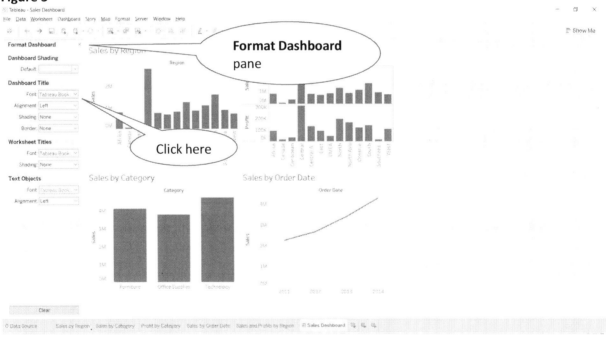

- Click the **Font** pulldown arrow as shown on Figure 3, which will popup the box displayed on Figure 4

Figure 4

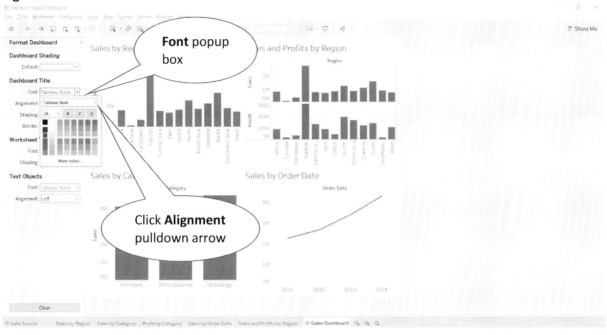

The **Font** popup box enables any desired changes to be made to the dashboard title (font type, size and colors). No font changes have been made in this step, which is for information purpose only.

To change the **Alignment**:

- Click the **Alignment** pulldown arrow shown on Figure 5

Figure 5

Clicking the **Alignment** pulldown arrow shown on Figure 5 will lead to Figure 6 (where the alignment options are displayed).

Figure 6

No alignment changes have been made in this step, which is for information purpose only.

To change the **Shading**:
- Click the **Shading** pulldown arrow shown on Figure 7

Figure 7

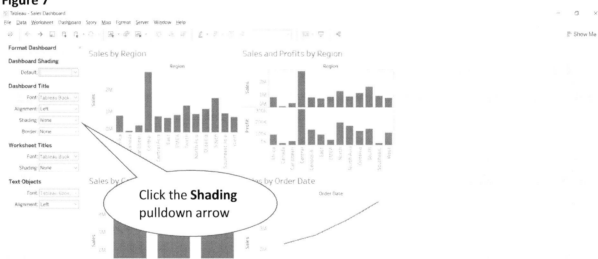

Clicking the **Shading** pulldown arrow shown on Figure 7 will lead to Figure 8 (where the shading options are displayed).

Figure 8

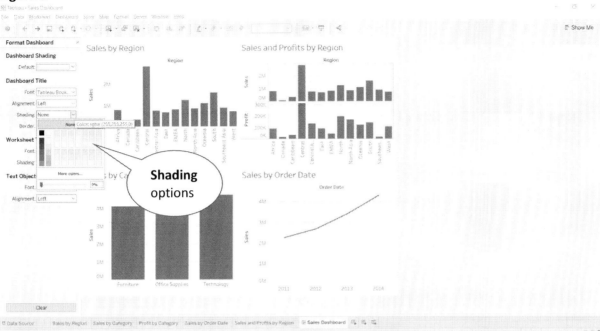

No shading changes have been made in this step, which is for information purpose only.

Figure 9 displays the **Sales Dashboard**. In the following steps, this dashboard will be formatted and a link to an external website will be incorporated in it.

Figure 9

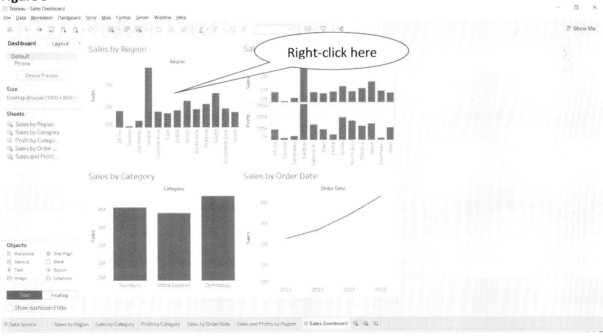

To reformat:

- Right click in the view to be modified (**Sales by Region**), which will popup the menu tree displayed on Figure 10

Figure 10

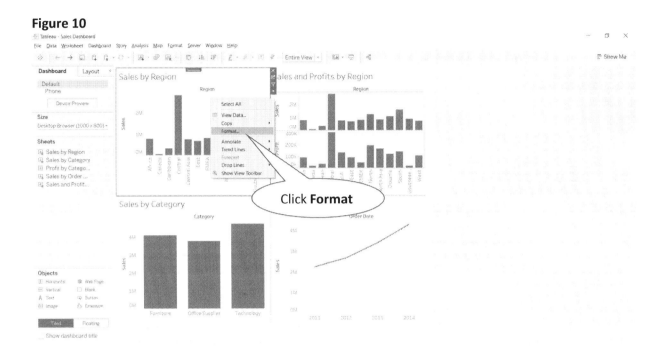

- Click **Format** as shown on Figure 10, which will popup the **Format Font** pane displayed on Figure 11 (on the left-hand side)

Figure 11

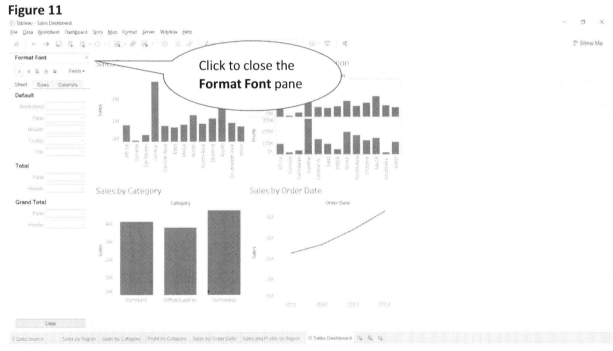

A wide range of formatting changes can be made on the **Format Pane** window, which is located on the left-hand side of the dashboard. This pane provides the option to make changes for a **Sheet, Rows** or **Columns**. Any one of these can be selected by clicking on the appropriate tab.

Web pages, which can provide easy access to external websites, can be easily added to a dashboard. We will add a website URL to Figure 12 **(Sales Dashboard).**

Figure 12

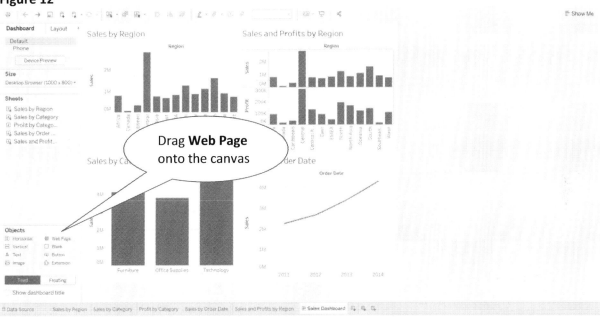

To add a **Web Page**:
- Drag the **Web Page** icon to the dashboard canvas as shown on Figure 12, which will lead to Figure 13

Figure 13

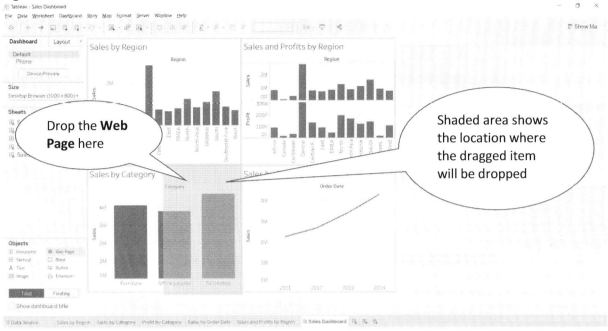

The shaded area on Figure 13 shows the location where the dragged item will be dropped. You can move this shaded area to any other desired spot before dropping the web page item.

- Drop the **Web Page** item at the desired canvas location as shown on Figure 13, which will popup the **Edit URL** box displayed on Figure 14

Figure 14

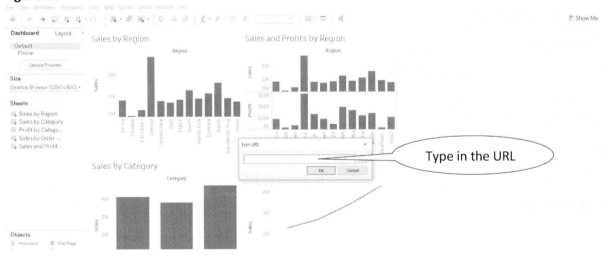

- Type in the **URL** (www.bing.com) in the **Edit URL** popup box as shown on Figure 14, which will lead to Figure 15

Figure 15

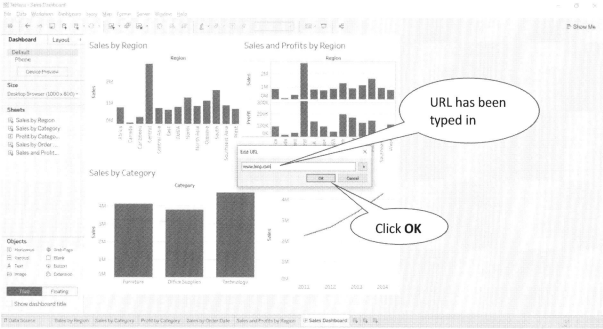

URL has been typed in

Click **OK**

- Click **OK**, which will add the URL and lead to Figure 16, where the **Bing** website is displayed

Figure 16

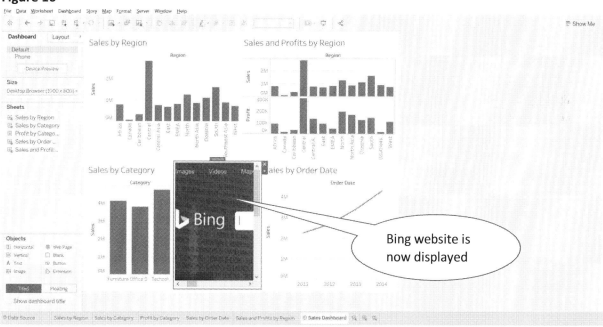

Bing website is now displayed

The individual views in this dashboard can be sized or moved, as desired.

Made in the USA
Las Vegas, NV
12 June 2022

50146066R00133